MAN OR WOMAN
BOY OR GIRL
THAT READS WHAT
FOLLOWS
3 TIMES
SHALL FALL ASLEEP
AN HUNDRED YEARS

JOHN D. BATTEN DREW THIS : AUG 29ᵀᴴ 1891   GOOD-NIGHT.

BOOKS BY JUDY SIERRA

Cinderella
Fantastic Theater
The Flannel Board Storytelling Book

WITH BOB KAMINSKI

Multicultural Folktales
Twice Upon a Time
Children's Traditional Games

FOR CHILDREN

Nursery Tales Around the World
Wiley and the Hairy Man
Goodnight, Dinosaurs
The House That Drac Built
Quests and Spells
The Elephant's Wrestling Match

STORYTELLERS' RESEARCH GUIDE

Folktales, myths and legends

JUDY SIERRA, PH.D

folkprint

eugene, oregon

Published in the United States of America by

FOLKPRINT

POST OFFICE BOX 450
EUGENE, OR 97440
(541) 683-9752

Manufactured in the United States of America

Copies of this guide may be ordered from the publisher for $14.95 plus $3.00 shipping and handling. Inquire via e-mail for foreign rates: sierra@continet.com.

BOOK AND COVER DESIGN BY JUDY SIERRA

Frontispiece: A drawing by John D. Batten that appeared preceding the notes section of Joseph Jacobs' *Celtic Fairy Tales* (1892).

Rock art on the front cover from the Columbia River area

LCCN: 96-986625

This guide is updated
on the World Wide Web:
http://www.continet.com/folkprint

CONTENTS

INTRODUCTION

It is customary for a person who goes on a long voyage to tell the story of the journey upon her return. I recently traveled to the realms of academia in order to earn a Ph.D. in Folklore and Mythology. The trip was often difficult for a performing artist who was used to improvising, stretching the truth, and relying as much on intuition as on documentation. I returned from my voyage with a traveler's desire to share what I saw and what I learned, and so I offer this guide to storytellers who, like me, want to further explore the world of tales and the oral tradition. Although it is intended primarily for those who tell stories to live audiences, this book will also be useful to editors, authors, illustrators and teachers who use traditional tales in their work.

There is a wealth of tale texts and related material available to the storyteller, but locating them can be difficult. In this guide, I provide selected bibliographies and suggest research strategies to assist in the quest. *Chapter 1: Research Basics* includes a survey of library and online resources, and describes in detail how to find material using electronic catalogs and indexes. Those in need of ready-to-tell tales will find recommended anthologies and bibliographies in *Chapter 2: Tellable Tales*. Storytellers who want to locate a specific tale, or lesser-known tales or tale variants will find resources, including a bibliography of tale type and motif indexes, in *Chapter 3: Tracking Down Tales*. Bibliographies and other tools for locating cultural background information can be found in *Chapter 4: Around and About the Tale.* *Chapter 5: Fieldwork* offers an introduction to collecting tales and tale-related material from real live folks. *Chapter 6: Copyright for Storytellers* explains copyright and the public domain, including when, why and how to request permission to tell a tale.

In selecting material to include in this book, I have used two criteria: each book, article, or other work must reflect a sound knowledge of folklore and related fields and must also be practical and useful to a storyteller. One of my main objectives in creating this guide has been to point out relevant, readable academic and scholarly works that a storyteller might otherwise overlook. Because storytellers have such diverse needs and interests, I could never list every important book and article, so I have tried to select those works that will point the way, through indexes, source notes and bibliographies, to other more specialized resources.

In order to standardize the bibliographies, I have listed tale collections alphabetically by the name of the compiler, omitting the terms editor, compiler, translator, etc. Also, because this entire guide is essentially a bibliographic essay, there is no general bibliography. The author and short title indexes can be used to locate full bibliographic citations.

Acknowledgements

I owe an enormous debt to the faculty of the Folklore and Mythology Program of the University of California, Los Angeles, especially Donald Ward, Joseph Nagy, Michael Owen Jones, Robert Georges, and Donald Cosentino. I offer my sincerest thanks as well to friends who offered advice and encouragement: Judith O'Malley, Leslie Jones, Margaret Read Macdonald, Barbara Stevens-Newcomb, Jeff Defty, Ruth Stotter, and Bob Kaminski—and to Bruce Carrick, whose request that I find twenty-four folktales in the public domain sent me to the UCLA library, and started it all.

CHAPTER ONE

RESEARCH BASICS

The terms used to describe tales that have been shaped and passed on orally—myth, folktale, legend, epic, tall tale, fable, etc.—are everyday words. Unfortunately, they are not used in a consistent way either in conversation, in scholarly books, or in library catalogs. Folklorists use the general terms *oral narrative* and *folk narrative* to describe tales that follow traditional patterns. Within the oral narrative tradition, folklorists have developed fairly standard divisions and definitions of genres and subgenres. The following are those that are most relevant to contemporary storytellers.

Folktale designates a narrative that people in the originating culture consider fiction. Like literary fiction, the folktale requires a willing suspension of disbelief on the part of listeners. Folktales are often marked by traditional opening and closing formulas, and by a style that differs from that of ordinary conversation. The major subgenres of the folktale are:

Fable. A brief tale, often with animal protagonists, that illustrates an ethical or moral teaching.

Fairy tale, also known as wonder tale or by the German term, *Märchen*. A tale about a young person's transition from childhood to adulthood, usually represented by marriage. Magical beings, animals and objects figure prominently in fairy tales.

Formula tale. A brief tale in which a mechanical, highly predictable plot structure is foregrounded.

Joke. A short narrative in which an unexpected twist at the end provokes laughter.

Numskull tale. A lighthearted tale of extremely foolish behavior.

Tall tale. A tale which relies on outrageous exaggeration and lying for its comic effect.

Legend. A fictional or partly fictional narrative that is told as if it were true. Legends were believed by at least some of the original tellers and listeners. Though a legend might appear at first to be factual and unique, upon investigation it is found to have a traditional plot. Some types of legend preferred by contemporary storytellers are:

Supernatural legend. A tale in which mysterious and fantastic beings, including the dead, interact with people much like ourselves.

Urban legend. A contemporary tale of strange and troubling events, usually claimed to have happened to a "friend of a friend."

Historical legend. A fictional or partly fictional tale about real people and real events.

Myth. A narrative that is considered both true and sacred in the originating culture. Not all myths are told as complete stories. They are often conveyed piecemeal in epics, legends, rituals, the visual art, etc.

Epic. A long tale in many episodes which relates the exploits of exceptional figures such as Beowulf and Gilgamesh. Purely oral epics have been recorded in many cultures, and the epic form is also common in literature.

This division into genres works most successfully with tales of European origin, but even there, it tends to break down under close scrutiny. For example, European tellers of fairy tales often expressed a belief in them, although fairy tales are classified as folktales, which are supposed to be recognized by tellers and listeners as fiction. In spite of any shortcomings, however, an understanding of genre distinctions can help a teller select and prepare stories and understand audience response.

The genre most readily appreciated across cultures is the folktale, and especially tales about human foibles and virtues (these tales can feature either human or talking animal protagonists). Many trickster tales, numskull tales, and formula tales fall into this category, as do the oral traditional teaching tales of various religions. Folklorists Linda Dégh, who studied traditional Hungarian storytellers over several decades, noted that folktales were performed in a stylized way, while legends were simply related in a conversational manner.

Storytellers are faced with an interesting problem when telling legends to contemporary audiences. Legends derive their narrative appeal from being told as true, yet tellers, being educated in folklore, realize they are not true. Telling legends requires a careful negotiation with listeners so that they do not feel they have been tricked into believing a tale they later discover is false. Yet if teller and listeners agree that the legend is fiction, it becomes a folktale, and requires the structure and patterning typical of that genre.

Many contemporary storytellers seek out myths in the belief that they are powerful vehicles for exploring meaning. They may be shocked to discover that many of the world's myths are as violent and sexually explicit as any contemporary popular entertainment. The Greek myths are a case in point. Myth is also the tale genre that is most likely to be incomprehensible to the uninitiated. Most myths have as their purpose the justification of a social order that is far from universal or natural, such as one group or one gender dominating another. Adapting myths for contemporary audiences poses a real challenge to the storyteller. Taken out of cultural context and altered to appease potential censors, myths become marginally interesting stories that are important only because they are marketed as "sacred tales from such and such a culture."

Contemporary storytellers should not mistake a folktale with an etiological ending for a myth. "How and why" stories—ones that end with ". . . and that is why the sun and moon are in the sky," or a similar phrase connecting the tale to a fact of everyday life—are not necesssarily sacred tales. It is more likely that they are simply folktales, conveying their own sort of truth and wisdom, of course, but not myths, and certainly not believed to be true by any but the youngest listeners. These endings are usually just playful closing formulas, and in some communities, different storytellers tell the same tale with a different how and why ending.

Research tools and skills

Researching oral traditional tales is both exhilarating and challenging. If you are simply looking for new tales to tell, you should be able to find all the resources you need in a medium-sized public library. However, if you wish to research the narrative traditions of a certain region or ethnic group, if you are looking for variants of a tale, or for lesser-known tales, you will probably need to use a major public library, or a college or university library. Access to the Internet will allow you to search library catalogs and periodical indexes from home, and to contact other storytellers for advice and assistance.

Good library research habits will save you time and frustration. Keep a notebook in which you record the sources you want to examine, or have examined, and their location (library and call number). Note the name of each bibliography and index you have searched, and the subject headings and keywords you used. This will save you the unpleasant task of having to repeat your work. A good, legible record of your search will be invaluable if you need to ask a librarian for help.

A knowledge of several languages, or friends and associates who can assist you with translation, is an enormous asset in tale research. The two major languages of international folklore scholarship are German and English, and some of the important German works have not been translated, *e.g.*, the *Enzyklopädie des Märchens*, a multivolume encyclopedia covering all aspects of oral narrative and storytelling. The availability of tales in English depends upon who collected them and whether translators, editors and publishers took an interest in them. There are large numbers of tales available in English from the parts of the world colonized by the British or favored by English-speaking anthropologists. The number of English translations of texts from other regions, including much of Asia, is relatively small.

Know thy librarians

Reference librarians can be valuable research partners. A good librarian will assist you by suggesting research strategies, consulting reference books, performing online searches, and posting difficult questions to specialized discussion groups. Not all librarians are equally resourceful and helpful, and you may need to do some investigative work in order to locate the best ones. Get to know children's librarians, who often are storytellers themselves. Librarians, especially in public libraries, are accustomed to dealing with impatient people, who want reference questions answered immediately or not at all. If you are willing to wait a few days or a few weeks for an answer, make this clear to the librarian. Librarians can, if necessary, either refer difficult questions to regional reference centers, or post them to professional discussion groups on the Internet.

Public libraries

Public libraries in the United States have always had a special relationship with folklore, due in part to the long tradition of storytelling by children's librarians. Librarians purchase tale collections liberally, in both the children's and adult areas, and are reluctant to discard older, out-of-print volumes. Most storytellers head immediately for the shelves labeled 398 or 398.2, the basic Dewey Decimal classification numbers for folktales and legends. When browsing the shelves, don't neglect 290-299, religion and mythology; 372.64, storytelling, including tale collections especially for storytellers; and the 800's, literature, including some myths and epics.

Through interlibrary loan, libraries can borrow materials from other libraries nationwide. The cost of this service varies, and the trend is toward higher fees, though sometimes there is no charge. If you only need a part of a book (one tale from a collection, for example), the lending library may send a photocopy. Magazines and journals are seldom loaned, but again, photocopies are routinely sent. Many tale collections and tale type indexes are published as parts of monograph series, that is, they are books, but they are issued as a numbered series, usually by an academic institution or professional society. There are several important monograph series in folklore, including *Folklore Fellows Communications* and *Memoirs of the American Folklore Society.* Libraries often classify and shelve these monograph series as if they were journals, and may treat them like journals for the purposes of interlibrary loan, that is, refuse to lend them. If you are trying to obtain a volume of a monograph series through interlibrary loan, you may need to convince the borrowing or lending library that the work you need is really a book.

Academic libraries

With a few exceptions, college and university libraries in the U.S will allow anyone to use their general collections, and will issue library cards to members of the public for a fee. Academic libraries recognize independent researchers as an important clientele, and the fee you pay for your card should also entitle you to staff assistance. The hours of academic libraries vary according to the academic schedule. During school breaks libraries close earlier; however, it's usually easier then to park, to obtain help from the staff, and to find books on the shelf.

Academic libraries shelve their books according to the Library of Congress classification system, rather than the Dewey

Decimal System. The LC call numbers for folklore begin with GR (located conveniently between GN, anthropology, and GT, manners and customs). Native American tales are classified in history sections E and F, and mythology is located in BL.

Be aware that the online catalog may not contain entries for all of an academic institution's holdings. Some libraries still keep a card catalog for older material. Also, a campus may have a number of separate libraries, including departmental libraries, and these catalogs may not be part of the main catalog. Works relevant to folklore might be housed in departments of folklore, anthropology, linguistics, literature, area studies, ethnic studies and in music and art libraries.

Special collections, special libraries, and archives

Special collections of books, media and manuscripts exist within public and academic libraries, and also in museums, historical societies, and foundations. For example, the Folklore Archive, located in the English Department of my local university (University of Oregon), contains a collection of reports of bigfoot sightings, a fact I discovered in the *Directory of Special Libraries and Information Centers*. The following are the major guides to special collections, special libraries and archives:

Ash, Lee, and William G. Miller, eds. *Subject Collections: A Guide to Special Book Collections and Subject Emphases as Reported by University, College, Public, and Special Libraries and Museums in the United States and Canada.* 7th ed. New York: R.R. Bowker, 1993.

Turecki, Gwen E., ed. *Directory of Special Libraries and Information Centers: A Guide to More than 22,400 Special Libraries, Research Libraries, Information Centers, Archives, and Data Centers Maintained by Government Agencies.* 19th ed. Detroit, Mich.: Gale Research, 1996.

World Guide to Special Libraries. 2nd ed. London: Saur, 1995.

There are also regional, state and local guides to special library collections. They can be found using the LC subject heading: Library resources -- [state, county, etc.] -- Directories.

Online library catalogs and periodical indexes

Most libraries in the U.S have online catalogs and periodical indexes accessible at computer work stations in the library, or offsite (*i.e.*, in your home) via modem. Online catalogs offer many more ways of searching than the old subject/author/title card catalogs. The following instructions for using online catalogs are general, since there are many different systems now in use. These systems offer similar search options, but the keystroke commands vary (maddeningly). Online catalogs allow searching for materials in several fields, or categories. You may also combine search terms and limit your searches in various ways. The full range of search options offered by a library catalog might not be apparent when viewing the initial screen; you may have to select a help screen, or similar option, in order to learn all the possibilities.

Keyword. Online catalogs allow searches of records by keyword, so that you no longer need to know the exact title of a book or the precise wording of a subject heading. In fact, many catalogs interpret any title or subject words as keywords. To perform a keyword search, simply enter two or three of the least common words in a particular title or subject heading.

Unfortunately for the tale researcher, the words folktale, myth and legend are used pretty much interchangeably in the titles of books and journal articles. And the word folktale has at various times been written folk tale and folk-tale. Scholars in some fields prefer to use the terms oral literature and folk literature rather than oral narrative and folk narrative. When you prepare to search catalogs and indexes by keyword, your list of search terms may need to include: folklore, folktales, folk tales, legends, myths, mythology, oral literature, folk literature, oral tradition, oral narrative, and folk narrative.

Subject headings. The Library of Congress produces an official list of subject headings, which is contained in several large volumes, and may also be searched through Locis, the Library of Congress online catalog, available via the World Wide Web at http://lcweb.loc.gov/ or http://www.loc.gov/ or by telnet at locis.loc.gov. Sadly, there is little rhyme or reason to the subject headings assigned to books of oral traditional tales. Official LC headings include: Tales, Legends, Mythology, Myths, Folk literature and Oral tradition.

In the LC subject heading lists, you will find cross references from the words an ordinary person would think of to words used by Library of Congress catalogers. I always try to identify and search using as many LC subject headings as possible. I often work backwards, first looking up a book on my subject that I already know, and seeing which subject headings the Library of Congress has assigned to it. I use those headings to search for similar books. I also search any title keywords I suspect an author would use in the title or subtitle of a book on my subject.

Notes. The notes or contents field provides some information about the contents of a work, and is searchable by keyword. It is available for some, though not all, recently-published books, audiotapes, and videotapes,. In the case of children's fiction and folktales, this field often contains a brief summary of the plot. The notes field also can include the table of contents of an anthology. The names of tellers and titles of tales on audiotape storytelling collections are searchable via the notes field.

Series. You can search for books in this field using a series title. If you are looking for several books in the same series, such as *Folktales of the World*, this can be a time-saver.

Truncation is the use of a part of a word to locate all words containing a specific string of letters. To indicate truncation, a symbol, such as * or $, is placed before or after the string of letters. An example of a truncated search would be a keyword search in either the title or subject field for storytell*. This search would locate titles and subject headings containing the words storyteller(s) and storytelling.

Limiting a search. In some catalogs and indexes, it is possible to limit a search so that you retrieve fewer irrelevant titles. When a search nets hundreds of items, limits may be a necessity rather than an option. Searches can be limited by language, year(s) of publication, and format. Language is self-explanatory. A limit on publication year can be used, for instance, to search only for the most recent publications on a subject, or for works old enough to be in the public domain. Using format limits, you could search solely for books, or audio-cassettes, or videos.

Boolean searching is a way of combining keywords using the operators *and, or, not, near,* etc. This can be useful or even necessary when searching a very large database such as the World Wide Web. Many Web browsers provide Boolean searching options. A full explanation of Boolean searching would be quite lengthy. A reference librarian can give you information on conducting this type of search.

Shelf browsing allows you to scroll through items onscreen, just as if you were looking through the library's shelves with nothing checked out. You can initiate shelf browsing either by entering a specific call number, or starting from the onscreen record of a particular book. The online catalog should also indicate whether an item is checked out or available for borrowing. If you are searching from outside the library, and want to make sure an item will still be on the shelf when you arrive, call ahead. Most public libraries will search for it and set it aside for you (academic libraries do not usually provide this service).

Other online resources

The online catalogs of many libraries also provide access to periodical indexes, and to other libraries' catalogs. Those who remember painstakingly searching through volume after volume of *Reader's Guide to Periodical Literature* will be delighted to be able to search this and similar indexes at a computer workstation. Unfortunately for the folklore researcher, coverage in online periodical databases generally begins in the 1980s, and no publisher I have queried has plans to convert older print indexes to electronic format. The *Modern Language Association Bibliography (MLA Bibliography)*, one of the most complete indexes of folklore in journals, books and dissertations, is available in electronic format from 1963 to date. Unlike other similar indexes however, it does not include any abstracts. Commercial services such as CARL UNcover not only index periodicals but will, for a fee, deliver copies of articles via mail or fax. There is a trend toward access to abstracts and full text of articles online and toward the electronic publication of journals.

Be aware that the search commands and subject headings of periodical indexes are probably different from those of the main library catalog, and from each other. Most indexes have their own specialized list of *descriptors,* or subject keywords. You may be able to access this list (a *thesaurus*) onscreen, or it may only be available in printed form. The lack of standards among electronic reference tools can be very frustrating.

The largest online library catalogs of them all are WorldCat, a commercial service which boasts 34 million entries, and Locis, the U.S. Library of Congress catalog, which contains a mere 27 million items. You may access Locis free of charge by telnetting to locis.loc.gov, or via the Web at http://www.loc.gov/ or http://lcweb.loc.gov/. Subscribers to WorldCat pay a fee, and most individuals access this mega-catalog through their local public or university library. The Library of Congress' Locis is, at present, difficult to search, whereas WorldCat is very user-friendly. The WorldCat database is worldwide and retrospective. It can be used to ferret out obscure books on a subject, and to compile bibliographies.

The promises and limits of technology

The quality of folklore and mythology resources varies widely. Older publications are not necessarily out of date, and new works are not always well-researched or reliable. Although electronic indexing has made it possible for a researcher to access the catalogs of library collections worldwide, catalogs don't reveal much about the contents of a book or article, or evaluate its quality. Good bibliographies by subject specialists remain the researcher's best friends. Often these bibliographies are parts of larger works, and can only be located by patient searching in libraries, through other bibliographies, or by word of mouth.

There are wonderful tools available online for researchers— library catalogs, periodical indexes, newsgroups and discussion groups, newsletters, and an increasing number of academic journals. You will find very few tale texts, however, and of those, only a handful are genuine or interesting. This is due to copyright concerns and also to the cost of placing older texts online. Material protected by copyright (this includes nearly everything published in the U.S. in the past 75 years) cannot legally be placed online without permission of the copyright owner. Publishers currently have no incentive to do this, since there is not yet an accepted way to collect payment from end-users. The only printed documents that can be placed online easily are those that were typeset electronically, providing this data still exists. Other text can only be placed online if someone types it, or scans it using an optical character recognition program (this requires careful editing afterward). The Library of Congress is converting some historical documents to electronic format, at an estimated cost of three dollars per page.

When newer and better online sources become available, they should be findable through the Library of Congress Folklife Home Page (http://www.loc.gov/folklife/) and Harvard University's Folklore and Mythology Home Page (http://www.fas.harvard.edu/~folkmyth/).

Storytellers on the Internet

The Storytelling Home Page on the World Wide Web, http://members.aol.com/storypage/, is hosted by Jim Maroon, who is both a storyteller and a librarian. It is a model of a good web site: attractive (yet it doesn't take long to download), well-organized and easy-to-use. It provides links to many resources of interest, including a directory of storytelling groups in the U.S.

and Canada, storytellers' home pages, and listings of upcoming festivals.

Discussion groups (also known as listservs) and newsgroups allow you to pose questions and discuss topics of interest with others worldwide. To subscribe to a discussion group, you must have an e-mail address. To participate in Storytell, a discussion group for storytellers, e-mail the message "subscribe Yourfirstname Yourlastname" to storytell-request@venus.twu.edu. You'll receive tons of mail from this group's outspoken members. Be sure to save your first message from the listserv, which gives instructions for stopping the mail. The archive of Storytell may be searched by keyword. The address of the archive is long and filled with symbols. I suggest accessing it by way of the Storytelling Home Page.

Newsgroups are accessed via internet providers; you log on to read messages, rather than receiving them as e-mail, as you would with a listserv. There is a newsgroup for storytellers, alt.arts.storytelling. If you have questions concerning tales which may have been published in children's collections or told to children, try rec.arts.books.childrens, a newsgroup that includes many knowledgeable children's librarians and authors.

The Directory of Electronic Journals, Newsletters and Academic Discussion Lists, edited by Dru W. Mogge (6th ed. Washington, D.C.: Association of Research Libraries, 1996) is an excellent guide to online resources, arranged by subject.

CHAPTER TWO

TELLABLE TALES

Tales in books are not all suited to oral telling, as every storyteller soon discovers. Tales from the oral tradition have qualities that can best be described as "tellable." Not all of them, of course, yet a surprising number are easy to learn and permit even a relatively inexperienced storyteller to captivate an audience. Over the centuries, folk narratives have depended upon human memory for their survival, so they are structured in a way that makes best use of natural memory, as opposed to trained memory. Also, an individual tale is always part of a narrative tradition; the more tales a teller knows from a related group of tales (European fairy tales, for instance, or Anansi stories, or Brer Rabbit tales), the easier it is to learn a new one. Folktales are more likely to have a memorable structure than myths or legends. The subject matter and structure of folktales—the journey, the tasks to be fulfilled, repetition, cumulation—are mnemonic devices. All oral genres employ simple and striking visual images, which are easy to recall, and which fascinate listeners. Tellability is culturally relative too, of course. The themes of traditional tales are deeply ingrained in a culture, and vice-versa. For most people raised in a European culture, the Grimms' tales cling to the memory. Several storytellers have told me that they can read a Grimms' tale at night and tell it the next day. One writer has even called them a sort of memory virus!

Most literary stories, even those that are enchanting when read silently or aloud, lack tellability. The very qualities we value in fiction, such as originality of plot and style, precise language, and well-developed characters, only serve to flummox the real-time recall demanded of the storyteller. Still, contemporary storytellers do tell literary tales. Those with theater training can give a verbatim dramatization of a literary piece, though this is not really storytelling, that is, it lacks the impromptu shaping that distinguishes storytelling from acting. Other tellers artfully rework favorite literary pieces into an oral style. There are certain literary tales that have proven more tellable than others, and storytellers seem to prefer the tales of a few authors—Rudyard Kipling, Richard Kennedy, and Judith Gorog, for example. I have noted which of the bibliographies below include tried-and-true literary tales.

If you aren't convinced of the difference in tellability between oral and literary tales, try the Grimm (more oral) vs. Andersen (more literary) test. Choose one tale from each collection that is well-known, preferably one that hasn't been made into a Disney film—for example, "Hansel and Gretel" from the Grimms' tales, and "The Ugly Duckling" by Hans Christian Andersen. Grab a willing listener and try to tell both tales. You can read through the texts first, or not, as you choose. Even if you recall only the bare essentials of each tale, you'll find that it is easier to retell and improvise upon an oral than a literary text.

Some anthologists are famous among storytellers for their very tellable tales, while others are not. What accounts for the difference? Two 19th century folklore scholars, Andrew Lang and Joseph Jacobs, are good examples. As a child, I treasured the Lang colored fairy book series. As a storyteller, give me Jacobs any day! Andrew Lang identified tales in published collections from various countries, and engaged friends and associates to translate them into English. Many of the tales in the Lang collections are literary reworkings of folk tradition, and some do not come from the folk tradition at all. Joseph Jacobs loved to tell stories himself. His editorial technique, which he described in the endnotes of his anthologies, was to combine several versions of the same tale to create a telling that pleased him. Jacobs' story language has cadence and charm, and his tales are easy to learn and still delight audiences a century after they were published. Jacobs' four very tellable collections are from the English and Irish traditions, both of which Jacobs knew from childhood, while his collections of tales from the European continent and India are, well, forgettable.

The tales that are most tellable are not verbatim transcriptions of performances by traditional storytellers. Even the most skilled narrator has lapses in memory, and doesn't always say things in the best way tradition has to offer. Tellable tales are literate, artistic reworkings of traditional material. They combine the best elements of many tale variants to produce a scenario from which a storyteller can create a new performance.

The following is a selective list of the most useful tale anthologies and bibliographies for beginning storytellers, and for any tellers who don't have much time to research and learn tales. The most tellable tales are not the shortest, nor the sweetest, nor those with the worthiest moral or message. Their workings are mysterious, and they must be told in order to be fully appreciated. A beginner will avoid disappointment and frustration by choosing tales from recommended anthologies and bibliographies, and by asking experienced storytellers for recommendations.

Tale collections especially for storytellers

Baltuck, Naomi. *Apples from Heaven: Multicultural Tales About Stories and Storytellers.* North Haven, Conn.: Linnet Books, 1995.

Best-Loved Stories Told at the National Storytelling Festival. Little Rock, Ark.: August House, 1991; *More Best-Loved Stories Told at the National Storytelling Festival.* Little Rock, Ark.: August House, 1992.

These tales from nationally-recognized tellers will help a beginner understand the kind of storytelling that engages and delights adult audiences. Many of the tales in these books are also available on a series of audiocasettes from the National Storytelling Association.

Holt, David, and Bill Mooney. *Ready-to-Tell Tales.* Little Rock, Ark.: August House, 1994.

Forty-one tales by many of the best-known contemporary tellers. Most were recorded first on the tellers' audiotapes, which are listed in the book.

Joining In: An Anthology of Audience Participation Stories and How to Tell Them. Cambridge, Mass.: Yellow Moon Press, 1985.

Participation tales contributed by many storytellers, along with instructions for including the audience in the telling.

MacDonald, Margaret Read. *Twenty Tellable Tales: Audience Participation Folktales for the Beginning Storyteller.* Bronx, N.Y.: H.W. Wilson, 1986.

MacDonald's versions of folktales feature the chants and repetition that young children adore. The tales are typeset in an "ethnopoetic" format, a sort of performance score that helps beginners achieve an engaging storytelling style. Other similar collections by MacDonald include: *Celebrate the World: Twenty Tellable Folktales for Multicultural Festivals,* Bronx, N.Y.: H.W. Wilson, 1994; *Look Back and See: Twenty Lively Tales for Gentle Tellers,* Bronx, N.Y.: H.W. Wilson, 1991; *Storyteller's Start-Up Book: Finding, Learning, Performing and Using Folktales, Including 12 Tellable Tales,* Little Rock, Ark.: August House, 1993; *When the Lights Go Out: Twenty Scary Tales to Tell,* Bronx, N.Y.: H.W. Wilson Co., 1988.

Pellowski, Anne. *The Story Vine: A Source Book of Unusual And Easy-To-Tell Stories from Around the World.* New York: Macmillan, 1984.

This collection features traditional activities to use while telling, such as string figures and paper folding.

Sierra, Judy and Robert Kaminski. *Twice Upon a Time: Stories to Tell, Retell, Act Out, and Write About*. Bronx, N.Y.: H.W. Wilson, 1989.

An anthology of twenty folktales that appeal to children ages 7-12, along with related puppetry, creative drama and writing projects. Other books by Robert Kaminski and Judy Sierra: *Multicultural Folktales for Feltboard and Readers' Theater*, Phoenix, Ariz.: Oryx Press, 1996; *Multicultural Folktales: Stories to Tell Young Children*, Phoenix, Ariz.: Oryx Press, 1991.

Tashjian, Virginia. *Juba This and Juba That: Story Hour Stretches for Large and Small Groups*. Boston: Little, Brown, 1995, 1969; *With a Deep Sea Smile: Story Hour Stretches for Large and Small Groups*. Boston: Little, Brown, 1974.

Funny stories, silly stories, and instant participation stories.

Yolen, Jane. *Favorite Folktales from Around the World*. New York: Pantheon Books, 1986.

A storyteller's choice of tales appropriate for children, adults, and mixed audiences.

Regional treasuries for the storyteller

Abrahams, Roger D. *African Folktales: Traditional Stories of the Black World*. New York: Pantheon Books, 1983.

—. *Afro-American Folktales: Stories from Black Traditions in the New World*. New York: Pantheon Books, 1985.

Afanasev, Aleksandr Nikolaevich. *Russian Fairy Tales*. New York: Pantheon Books, 1945.

Asbjornsen, Peter Christen, and Jorgen Moe. *Popular Tales from the Norse*. Edinburgh: Edmonston and Douglas, 1859.

Bushnaq, Inea. *Arab Folktales.* New York: Pantheon Books, 1986.

Calvino, Italo. *Italian Folktales.* New York: Pantheon Books, 1980.

Chase, Richard. *Grandfather Tales: American-English Folk Tales.* Boston: Houghton Mifflin, 1948.

—*Jack Tales.* Boston: Houghton Mifflin, 1943.

Courlander, Harold. *The Hat-Shaking Dance, and Other Ashanti Tales from Ghana.* New York: Harcourt Brace, 1957.

> Some other Courlander collections filled with tellable tales include: *The Fire on the Mountain, and Other Stories from Ethiopia and Eritrea,* New York: Holt, 1950; *Kantchil's Lime Pit and Other Stories from Indonesia,* New York: Harcourt Brace, 1950; *The King's Drum, and Other African Stories,* New York: Harcourt Brace, 1962; *The Tiger's Whisker, and Other Tales and Legends from Asia and the Pacific,* New York: Harcourt Brace, 1959.

Erdoes, Richard and Alfonso Ortiz. *American Indian Myths and Legends.* New York: Pantheon Books, 1986.

Grimm, Jacob and Wilhelm. *The Complete Grimms' Fairy Tales.* New York: Pantheon, 1972.

Hamilton, Virginia. *The People Could Fly: American Black Folktales.* New York: Knopf, 1985.

Jacobs, Joseph. *English Fairy Tales.* New York: G.P. Putnam's Sons, 1898.

> Jacobs' other tellable collections are *Celtic Fairy Tales,* New York: G.P. Putnam's Sons, 1892; *More Celtic Fairy Tales,* London: David Nutt, 1894; *More English Fairy Tales,* London: David Nutt, 1894.

Robinson, Adjai. *Singing Tales of Africa.* New York: Scribner's, 1974.

Includes words and musical notation for songs to be sung during the storytelling.

Shah, Idries. *World Tales*. Harcourt Brace, 1979.

Shah's collections of Sufi tales also have oral structure.

Wolkstein, Diane. *The Magic Orange Tree and Other Haitian Folktales*. New York: Knopf, 1978.

Storyteller Wolkstein collected these tales from traditional tellers in Haiti. She includes songs (with notation), chants, and information about the tellers.

Especially for children

Among retellers of tales for children (and for adults who enjoy the simpler folktales), those whose work has proven especially tellable include Joe Hayes for tales from the American Southwest; Yoshiko Uchida for Japanese tales; Molly Bang for Asian tales; Arthur Ransome for Russian tales; Isaac Bashevis Singer and Steve Sanfield for Yiddish tales; Barbara Walker for Turkish tales; Seumas MacManus for Irish tales; Sorche nic Leodhas for Scottish tales; Alvin Schwartz for various tales, including his ever-popular *Scary Stories to Tell in the Dark* series; Julius Lester for African-American tales; Ashley Bryant for African and African-American tales; Verna Aardema for African tales; and Joseph Bruchac and John Bierhorst for Native tales of the Americas.

Some storytellers swear that the best way to learn a tale is to read a picture book version to children. Others swear that reading picture books to children *is* storytelling. Most children's librarians and teachers tell-and-read picture books in a way that resembles such traditional storytelling techniques as the Japanese *kamishibai*. Holding the book to one side, they glance occasionally at the text, commenting and improvising whenever they wish. A good recent bibliography of the 200 best folktale picture books for group sharing can be found in Judy Freeman's *Books Kids Will Sit Still For,* 2nd ed., New York: R.R. Bowker, 1995.

Thematic collections of tellable tales

Clarkson, Atelia and Gilbert B. Cross. *World Folktales.* New York: Scribner's, 1980.

> This collection Includes sixty-six folktales, representing a wide range of folktale themes. A bibliography of variants, with tale type and motif numbers, is included for each tale.

Creeden, Sharon. *Fair is Fair: World Folktales of Justice.* Little Rock, Ark.: August House, 1994.

Forest, Heather. *Wisdom Tales from around the World.* Little Rock, Ark.: August House, 1996.

—. *Wonder Tales from Around the World.* Little Rock, Ark.: August House, 1995.

Hamilton, Virginia. *In the Beginning: Creation Stories from Around the World.* San Diego: Harcourt Brace, 1988.

Hearne, Betsy. *Beauties and Beasts.* Phoneix, Ariz.: Oryx, 1993.

> A multicultural anthology of 27 tales like "Beauty and the Beast," with an extensive bibliography of additional variants.

Hodges, Margaret. *Hauntings: Ghosts and Ghouls from Around the World.* New York: Kingfisher, 1992.

Leach, Maria. *Noodles, Nitwits, and Numskulls.* Cleveland: World, 1961.

—. *The Thing at the Foot of the Bed.* Cleveland: Collins-World, 1959.

Littledale, Freya. *Ghosts and Spirits of Many Lands.* Garden City, N.Y.: Doubleday, 1970.

MacDonald, Margaret Read. *Peace Tales: World Folktales to Talk About.* Hamden, Conn.: Linnet Books, 1992.

—. *Tom Thumb.* Phoenix, Ariz.: Oryx, 1993.

> A multicultural collection of 25 tales of very small heroes and heroines. Notes to each tale cite several variants.

Shannon, George. *A Knock at the Door.* Phoenix, Ariz.: Oryx, 1992.

> A multicultural collection of 35 tales like the Grimms' "The Wolf and the Seven Little Kids," including a bibliography of related variants for each tale.

——. *Stories to Solve: Folktales from Around the World.* New York: Greenwillow, 1985.

> These folktales are arranged so that there is a question posed at the end for the listener to answer. Sequels: *More Stories to Solve: Fifteen Folktales from Around the World,* Greenwillow, 1990; *Still More Stories to Solve: Fourteen Folktales from Around the World,* Greenwillow, 1994.

Pellowski, Anne. *Hidden Stories in Plants: Unusual and Easy-to-Tell Stories from Around the World, Together with Creative Things to Do While Telling Them.* New York: Macmillan, 1990.

Phelps, Ethel Johnston. *Maid of the North: Feminist Folk Tales from Around the World.* New York: Holt, Rinehart, 1981.

——. *Tatterhood and Other Tales: Stories of Magic and Adventure.* Old Westbury, N.Y.: Feminist Press, 1978.

> Tales of adventuresome girls and strong women.

Sherman, Josepha. *Trickster Tales: 40 Folk Stories from Around the World.* Little Rock, Ark.: August House, 1996.

Sierra, Judy. Sierra, Judy. *Cinderella.* Phoneix, Ariz.: Oryx, 1992.

> A multicultural collection of 25 tales like Cinderella, with a bibliography of other variants.

——. *Nursery Tales around the World.* New York: Clarion Books, 1996.

> Eighteen tales in six thematic categories wuch as "Runaway Cookies," "The Victory of the Smallest," and "Fooling the Big Bad Wolf."

Spinning Tales, Weaving Hope: Stories of Peace, Justice and the Environment. Philadelphia: New Society Publishers, 1992.

Tellable tale lists in storytelling manuals

Breneman, Lucille N. and Bren Breneman. *Once Upon a Time: A Storytelling Handbook.* Chicago: Nelson-Hall, 1983.

> Includes an extensive bibliography of stories for an adult audience, many of them literary.

deVos, Gail. *Storytelling for Young Adults: Techniques and Treasury.* Engelwood, Co.: Libraries Unlimited, 1991.

> The excellent annotated bibliography of folk and literary material to tell teenagers is indexed by culture and theme.

Greene, Ellin, and Augusta Baker. *Storytelling: Art and Technique.* 3rd ed. New York: Bowker, 1996.

> The bibliography in this book was shaped by a century of storytelling at the New York Public Library. Tales are classified by age of audience, and include tried and true literary stories. See also the pamphlet *Stories: A List of Stories to Tell and Read Aloud.* 8th ed. New York: New York Public Library, 1990.

Schimmel, Nancy. *Just Enough to Make a Story; A Sourcebook for Storytelling.* 3rd ed. Berkeley, Ca.: Sisters' Choice Press, 1992.

> Tales in the bibliographies are tried-and-true, with emphasis on tales of peace and justice, and of independent girls and women.

Learning tellable tales firsthand

Many of today's storytellers learn tales the old-fashioned way—by listening to other storytellers. The ability to listen to a tale told, then reshape it in one's own mind and retell it, without ever looking at the tale in print, is a skill that storytellers seem to develop without really trying. In doing so, they are like-traditional storytellers such as Sean Ó Conaill of Ireland who claimed "I never heard a Finn-tale from the time I was a twelve-year-old boy, that I did not have in my head as soon as it was told." When you do hear a tale that sticks in your mind, and you feel that you want to tell it, be sure to talk to the storyteller first. You will want to know the source of the tale and receive permission to use it (see *Chapter 6: Copyright for Storytellers*).

Other storytellers are often the best source of recommendations for tellable tales. The Storytell discussion group (see page 15) is an excellent place to post inquiries, especially if you are looking for specific kinds of tales. You can search Storytell's archives of previous postings by keyword. The archives can be reached via the Storytelling Home Page on the World Wide Web (http://members.aol.com/storypage). Inquire at your public library about storytelling groups in your area, or find them in the latest edition of the *National Storytelling Directory,* published by the National Storytelling Association, P.O. Box 309, Jonesboro, Tennessee 37659 (tel. 423-753-2171).

CHAPTER THREE

TRACKING DOWN TALES

When you begin searching for tales, it's important to realize that there is no one authoritative or original version of a tale from the oral tradition. Individual tales exist as variants—each is one of many possible versions of a plot, or of a bundle of character types, images and episodes. For the general public, certain writers' and editors' versions of oral traditional tales have come to represent an entire type—the Grimms' "Hansel and Gretel," Charles Perrault's "Cinderella," and Joseph Jacobs' "Jack and the Beanstalk." In some cases, the best-known version of a tale type contradicts tradition. Charles Perrault's "Little Red Riding Hood" is an example. In oral variants collected in France, the child nearly always escapes by her own cleverness rather than being rescued by an adult.

A search for a specific tale may lead you instead to a similar one, or even to several related tales. Folklorists call the basic, distinct patterns of traditional narratives *tale types,* and many tales that together make up a tale type *variants*. Variants of a tale type are not simply the same story with different settings and character names. Tales of the same type can vary to a far greater degree than that, yet remain recognizably similar. Tales are remarkable for their variation and for their stability over time, and often across a wide geographical area. For examples of this phenomenon, read of the tale synopses in Marian Roalfe Cox's *Cinderella: Three Hundred and Forty-Five Variants of Cinderella, Catskin, and Cap o' Rushes* or in William Bascom's *African Folktales in the New World*.

How traditional tales got into print

When you read tales in books and journals, you may wonder how they came to be written down. Some collectors provide this information, others do not. Texts were transcribed by folklorists, anthropologists, linguists, teachers, colonial officials, missionaries, and even by traditional storytellers themselves. A tale collector may have grown up in the culture, and have heard similar tales since childhood; these collections are very valuable. In a lot of cases, though, the person recording the tale was an outsider to the culture. Some collectors observed actual storytelling sessions, while others simply elicited summaries of tales during interviews. Most experienced contemporary storyteller have a sixth sense concerning the authenticity of tales in collections; in many cases, a book's introduction and notes will help you evaluate the motive and methods of collectors and retellers.

Before the appearance of Jacob and Wilhelm Grimm's *Household Tales* in 1812, relatively few folktales had been published. Traditional oral tales were considered unworthy of the attention of scholars. A handful of authors such as Charles Perrault in France, Giambattista Basile in Italy, and Geoffrey Chaucer in England had retold familiar tales as literary works, but after the Grimms, there was an explosion of tale collecting, first in Europe, then throughout the world, especially in European colonies. In England, tales, folksongs, superstitions, quaint customs, etc. were known as "popular antiquities," and were sought out as avidly as buried Roman treasure. Popular antiquities were published in local newspapers, and later in books and in journals such as *Folklore*. Transcripts of tales were stored in national archives throughout Europe. Folklore was an important source of ethnic identity among groups struggling for national autonomy. All too frequently, however, the tellers of the tales, and the circumstances of telling were not recorded.

Finding tales: beginning

Library catalogs can be used to find some individual tales. If a tale has been published as a children's picture book, it can be located by exact title or title keywords. A picture book retelling can be a valuable resource, even if the text is not suitable for storytelling, because picture book authors often cite their sources. Tales in newer anthologies can be searched by title or title keywords in a library catalog's notes field. Although only a few anthologies' contents are searchable through this field, I have had some success with this strategy. As a last resort, after searching the indexes below, look for anthologies that would logically include your tales, *i.e.,* collections from a certain country or culture, about a certain tale character, etc., using the LC subject headings Folklore, Tales, Folk literature, Oral tradition, Legends, Myths, Mythology + the name of the country, region, ethnic group or culture.

Indexes to tales in collections

Folktales, myths and legends are not as well indexed as other forms of short fiction, such as poetry, plays and short stories. There simply isn't a great demand for ways to locate them, except on the part of teachers and children's librarians. The following indexes are likely to be owned by public libraries:

Ashliman, D.L. *A Guide to Folktales in the English Language Based on the Aarne Thompson Classification System.* New York: Greenwood Press, 1987.

> An index to many well-known tale collections for adults, such as the *Folktales of the World* series from the University of Chicago Press. This work is organized by Aarne-Thompson tale type number (see page 35), and has subject and standard title indexing as well.

Eastman, Mary Huse. *Index to Fairy Tales, Myths and Legends.* 2nd rev. ed. Boston: F.W. Faxon, 1926.

—. *Index to Fairy Tales, Myths and Legends: First Supplement.* Boston: F.W. Faxon, 1937.

—. *Index to Fairy Tales, Myths and Legends: Second Supplement.* Boston: F.W. Faxon, 1952.

Ireland, Norma O. *Index to Fairy Tales 1949-1972: Including Folklore, Legends and Myths in Collections.* Metuchen, N.J.: Scarecrow, 1973.

—. *Index to Fairy Tales 1973-1977: Including Folklore, Legends and Myths in Collections.* Metuchen, N.J.: Scarecrow, 1985.

—, and Joseph Sprug. *Index to Fairy Tales 1978-1986: Including Folklore, Legends and Myths in Collections.* Metuchen, N.J.: Scarecrow, 1989.

Sprug, Joseph, and Norma O. Ireland. *Index to Fairy Tales 1987-1992: Including 310 Collections of Fairy Tales, Folktales, Myths and Legends.* Metuchen, N.J.: Scarecrow, 1994.

Long a standard reference series, and owned by many public and academic libraries, these volumes index folktales, fairy tales, legends, myths, epics, and some authored works of fantasy, mainly in collections intended for children. The first volume is of special interest to storytellers since most of the collections indexed are now in the public domain. Because the subject indexing is very general, and the choice of collections to index is not based on quality, these works lead the researcher to many irrelevant and uninteresting tales.

MacDonald, Margaret Read. *The Storytellers' Sourcebook: A Subject, Title, and Motif Index to Folklore Collections for Children.* Detroit: Gale Research/Neal Schuman, 1982.

This is an index to children's folktales in 556 collections and 389 picture books published between 1960 and 1980. MacDonald based her classification system on Stith

Thompson's *Motif-Index of Folk-Literature* (see page 35). Similar tales are grouped together, regardless of their geographic or cultural origin. This work is fascinating browsing for the storyteller, and has a detailed subject index that allows the reader to be fairly certain a tale is appropriate before setting out in search of it. Includes a tale title index, and geographic and ethnic indexes. This work is deservedly a favorite of storytellers.

Ziegler, Elsie. *Folklore: An Annotated Bibliography and Index to Single Editions.* Westwood, Mass.: F.W. Faxon Co., 1973.

This index is somewhat helpful in locating tales published as picture books. While many of the out-of-print tale anthologies indexed by Eastman and MacDonald can still be found on library shelves, the older out-of-print picture books indexed by Ziegler are likely to have worn out and been discarded.

Collective story memory

If you cannot locate the tale you are seeking using these basic indexes, it is probably time to call upon the collective memory of other storytellers. Through online discussion groups and newsgroups, you can reach a large number of tellers and librarians (see page 14-15 for the names and addresses of these groups). Librarians have have access to professional discussion groups where such questions can be posted in your behalf. Because so many librarians are also storytellers, these discussion groups are valuable resources.

Finding tales - advanced

Advanced research into traditional tales requires a library with a strong folklore collection. Only the largest libraries will own the resources you need. Before traveling to visit a particular library, you can evaluate its folklore collection via telnet or the World Wide Web (see page 13 for addresses, or inquire about access through your local public library's online catalog). Any library with a serious folklore collection will own all volumes of the *Journal of American Folklore* and *Folklore Fellows Communications*. Search the catalog by subject to assess the library's strength in your particular area of interest.

A first step in researching a particular tale, whether you are looking for a specific text, or variants, is to ascertain how scholars refer to it. Does it fit a tale type or motif number? Do scholars refer to tales like it by a standard name? The following works will help you discover whether this is the case.

Motif and tale type indexes

As early folklore scholars examined the texts of oral tales, they discovered that there seemed to be a limited number of basic tale plots. Tales could be grouped according to general-types, such as *The Search for the Lost Husband* (*e.g.,* "Cupid and Psyche," "East of the Sun, West of the Moon"). Several scholars attempted to develop a classification system for tales, and in 1910, Finnish folklorist Antti Aarne published a catalog of tale types that today remains the standard system for folktales of European and East Indian origin. Each tale type is basically a plot type, and is assigned both a number and a standard title, for example, Tale type 510A. *Cinderella*. American folklorist Stith Thompson revised Aarne's work and translated it into English as *The Types of the Folktale*.

For many years, folklorists believed that the existence of many variants of a tale type pointed to a single original tale, or archetype. They thought that if they gathered and studied all the variants of a tale, they could discover where and when it was first told. Some of the tale studies below, such as Anna Birgitta Rooth's *The Cinderella Cycle*, were attempts to do this. However, these historic-geographic studies never provided convincing evidence of the origin of any tale. Fortunately for storytellers, though, the quest for tale origins provided the impetus for the creation of specialized tale type and motif indexes that now can be used to locate individual tale texts.

Aarne, Antti, and Stith Thompson. *The Types of the Folktale: A Classification and Bibliography.* 2nd revision. Folklore Fellows Communications 184. Helsinki: Suomalainen Tiedeakatemia, 1961.

> *The Types of the Folktale* classifies folktales told by people in the geographical region extending from India to Ireland, along with the areas settled by those people. Each tale type has been assigned a number and a name, and in many cases, distinct subtypes are identified by letters, for example, Type 510A, *Cinderella,* and Type 510B, *The Dress of Gold, of Silver and of Stars.* Similar tales are grouped together, such as numbers 300-749, Tales of Magic (fairy tales), and 1000-1199, Tales of the Stupid Ogre. The work provides a plot synopsis or outline for each tale type, and cross references to the *Motif-Index.* Although commonly referred to as the "tale type index" this work wasn't designed to be a tool for locating tale texts, and only a relatively small group of tale collections are indexed. The division into tale types is fairly arbitrary: many field-collected fairy tales require five or six tale type numbers to fully describe their plots. However, Aarne and Thompson's work has stood the test of time, and has provided specialists and nonspecialists alike a way to talk about groups of similar tales. Thompson's book, *The Folktale* (New York: Holt, Rinehart, 1946) is a valuable aid to understanding the classification system.

Thompson, Stith. *Motif-Index of Folk-Literature: a Classification of Narrative Elements in Folktales, Ballads, Myths, Fables, Mediaeval Romances, Exempla, Fabliaux, Jest-Books, and Local Legends.* Revised. 6 vols. Bloomington: Indiana Univ. Press, 1955-8. Also available in CD-ROM format.

> Stith Thompson developed another classification system, one that is applicable worldwide to all types of traditional narratives, as well as early written literature. It is based not on plot, but on smaller units of narrative, which Thompson called motifs. A motif is an element that is typical of and

occurs frequently in traditional narratives. Motifs may be character types, magical objects or animals, episodes, or unique ways of structuring a tale, such as cumulative repetition. The *Motif-Index* contains the following major divisions: mythological; animals; tabu; magic; the dead; marvels; ogres; tests; the wise and the foolish; deceptions; reversal of fortune; ordaining the future; chance and fate; society; rewards and punishments; captives and fugitives; unnatural cruelty; sex; the nature of life; religion; traits of character; humor; and miscellaneous. The *Motif-Index* is modeled on the Library of Congress' classification system, using letters, numbers, decimal extensions, and a standard name, for example, B175.1, "Magic salmon carries hero over water," or F311, "Fairies adopt human child." Like the Library of Congress system, the *Motif-Index* is intended to be revised and expanded. After each motif entry tales containing that motif are cited, as well as any scholarly studies of that particular motif. The detailed index and many cross-references make it easy to use, and it is fascinating to browse, however it is not a particularly useful source for finding individual tales. For that, it is necessary to turn to the regional works based on the *Types of the Folktale* and the *Motif-Index.*

Regional tale type and motif indexes

The following are some of the major English-language tale type and motif indexes, and one each in German and French. The tale texts referred to in English-language indexes are not necessarily in English. Some of the indexes are based on *The Types of the Folktale,* some on the *Motif-Index.* A few authors have combined the two systems, while others have invented their own classifications. The best indexes not only include extensive bibliographical references, but also provide synopses or outlines of variants. Storytellers can use these indexes to locate tale texts, to verify that a tale or tale element is traditional in a culture, and to learn how a tale type varied. The bibliography of a tale type or motif index serves as a good bibliography of tale collections from that region.

NOTE: Most of these regional indexes do not include subject indexes. You will need to consult *The Types of the Folktale* and the *Motif-Index* in order to identify the tale type and motif numbers you are seeking.

Azzolina, David S., ed. *Tale Type- and Motif-Indexes: An Annotated Bibliography.* New York: Garland, 1987.

> A bibliography of tale type and motif indexes published through the mid-1980s, 186 works in all (though many of them index literary texts rather than oral traditional tales). Besides the English-language works that follow, Azzolina includes indexes in German of Chinese, Dutch, Finnish, Icelandic, Mongolian, Persian, Romanian and Turkish tales; in French of the Arabian Nights tales; in Dutch of Indonesian tales; in Spanish of tales from Ecuador; and native language indexes of tales from Belarus, Belgium, Bulgaria, Czechoslovakia, Denmark, Georgia, Greece, Hungary, Italy, Latvia, Lithuania, Poland, Russia, Sweden, and Ukraine.

Arewa, Erastus Ojo. *A Classification of the Folktales of the Northern East African Cattle Area by Types.* New York: Arno Press, 1980.

Baer, Florence E. *Sources and Analogues of the Uncle Remus Tales.* Folklore Fellows Communications 228. Helsinki: Suomalainen Tiedeakatemia, 1980.

Bascom, William. *African Folktales in the New World.* Bloomington: Indiana Univ. Press, 1992.

> A discussion, along with plot summaries, of tale-types which Bascom found to be uniquely African in origin.

Baughman, Ernest Warren. *Type and Motif-Index of the Folktales of England and North America.* Indiana Univ. Folklore Series, no. 20. The Hague: Mouton, 1966.

Bodker, Laurits. *Indian Animal Tales* [East Indian]. Folklore Fellows Communications 148. Helsinki: Suomalainen Tiedeakatemia, 1957.

Boggs, Ralph S. *Index of Spanish Folktales.* Folklore Fellows Communications 90. Helsinki: Suomalainen Tiedeakatemia, 1930.

Bolte, Johannes, and Georg Polivka. *Anmerkungen zu den Kinder- und Hausmärchen der Brüder Grimm.* 5 vols. Leipzig: Dieterich'sche Verlagsbuchhandlung, 1913-1932.

A study of folktales that focuses on the 225 tales in the Grimms' collection, and includes extensive bibliographies of similar tales in all languages. The bibliographies can be used by those who do not read German to locate early published variants, in all languages, of specific Grimms' tales.

Briggs, Katherine M. *A Dictionary of British Folk-Tales in the English Language.* 2 vols. in 4. London: Routledge and Kegan Paul, 1970-71.

Includes tale texts.

Choi, In-hak. *A Type Index of Korean Folktales.* Seoul: Myong Ji Univ., 1979.

Does not follow the Aarne-Thompson system.

Christiansen, Reidar Thoralf. *The Norwegian Fairytales: A Short Summary.* Fellows Communications 46. Helsinki: Suomalainen Tiedeakatemia, 1922.

Clarke, Kenneth W. "A Motif-Index of the Folktales of Culture Area V—West Africa." Ph.D. diss. Indiana Univ., 1958.

Delarue, Paul, and Marie-Louise Tenèze. *Le conte populaire français.* 4 vols. Paris: Érasme, 1957-1985.

Includes French language tales from Canada, the U.S. and the Caribbean.

El-Shamy, Hassan M. *Folk Traditions of the Arab World: A Guide to Motif Classification.* 2 vols. Bloomington: Indiana Univ. Press, 1995.

Flowers, Helen H. *A Classification of Folktales of the West Indies by Types and Motifs.* New York: Arno Press, 1980.

Haboucha, Reginetta. *Types and Motifs of the Judeo-Spanish Folktales.* New York: Garland, 1992.

Hansen, Terrence Leslie. *The Types of the Folktales in Cuba, Puerto Rico, the Dominican Republic and Spanish South America.* Univ. of California Folklore Studies, No. 8. Berkeley and Los Angeles: Univ. of California Press, 1957.

Hodne, Ornulf. *The Types of the Norwegian Folktale.* New York: Columbia Univ. Press, 1984.

Ikeda, Hiroko. *A Type and Motif Index of Japanese Folk-Literature.* Folklore Fellows Communications 209. Helsinki: Suomalainen Tiedeakatemia, 1971.

Jason, Heda. *Types of Indic Oral Tales: Supplement.* Folklore Fellows Communications 242. Helsinki: Suomalainen Tiedeakatemia, 1989.

—. "Types of Jewish-Oriental Tales." *Fabula* 7 (1965): 115-22.

—. *Types of Oral Tales in Israel.* Jerusalem: Israel Ethnographic Society, 1975.

Kirtley, Bacil F. *A Motif-Index of Traditional Polynesian Narratives.* New York: Arno Press, 1980.

Klipple, May Augusta. *African Folktales with Foreign Analogues.* New York: Garland, 1992.

Lambrecht, Winifred. "A Tale-Type Index for Central Africa." Ph.D. diss. Univ. of California, Berkeley, 1967.

Neuland, Lena. *Motif Index of Latvian Folktales and Legends.* Folklore Fellows Communications 229. Helsinki: Suomalainen Tiedeakatemia, 1981.

O Súilleabháin, Sean, and Reidar Thoralf Christiansen. *The Types of the Irish Folktale.* Folklore Fellows Communications 188. Helsinki: Suomalainen Tiedeakatemia, 1963.

Robe, Stanley Linn. *Index of Mexican Folktales, Including Narrative Texts from Mexico, Central America and the Hispanic United States.* Univ. of California Folklore Studies, No. 26. Berkeley and Los Angeles: Univ. of California Press, 1973.

Seki, Keigo. "Types of Japanese Folktales." *Asian Folklore Studies* 25 (1966), 1-220.

Taylor, Archer. "A Classification of Formula Tales." *Journal of American Folklore 46* (1933), 77-88.

Thompson, Stith, and Jonas Balys. *The Oral Tales of India.* Indiana Univ. Folklore Series, No. 10. Bloomington: Indiana Univ. Press, 1958.

Thompson, Stith, and Warren E. Roberts. *Types of Indic Oral Tales: India, Pakistan and Ceylon.* Folklore Fellows Communications 180. Helsinki: Suomalainen Tiedeakatemia, 1960.

Ting, Nai-Tung. *A Type Index of Chinese Folktales in the Oral Tradition and Major Works of Non-Religious Classical Literature.* Folklore Fellows Communications 223. Helsinki: Suomalainen Tiedeakatemia, 1978.

Waterman, Patricia P. *A Tale-Type Index of Australian Aboriginal Oral Narratives.* Folklore Fellows Communications 238. Helsinki: Suomalainen Tiedeakatemia, 1987.

Wilbert, Johannes and Karin Simoneau. *Folk Literature of South American Indians: General Index.* Los Angeles: UCLA Latin American Center Publications, Univ. of California,1992.

An index by motif number and subject keyword to Wilbert and Simonsen's 23-volume collection of tales from South American Indian tribes (see page 42).

Wycoco, Remedios S. "The Types of North American Indian Tales." Ph.D diss. Indiana Univ., 1951.

Yanagita Kunio Guide to the Japanese Folk Tale, ed. by Fanny Hagin Mayer. Bloomington: Indiana Univ. Press, 1948.

Does not follow the Aarne-Thompson system.

Tale collections indexed by tale type and motif numbers.

When an editor provides a tale type and/or motif index to a book's contents, the work of the tale researcher is greatly simplified. The following collections are widely available in public and academic libraries. In addition, many tale collections, especially scholarly works, include useful subject indexes to tales and their contents. Recent anthologies are likely to include motif and tale type numbers in tale notes, even if they do not provide an index.

The *Folktales of the World* series, published by the University of Chicago Press, is a folklorists' delight. The narrator and circumstances of collection are noted for every tale. Each volume is indexed by tale type, motif and subject. *Folktales of Chile,* by Yolando Pino Saavedra, 1967; *Folktales of China,* by Wolfram Eberhard, 1965; *Folktales of England,* by Katharine M. Briggs and Ruth L. Tongue, 1965; *Folktales of Egypt,* by Hasan M. El-Shamy, 1980; *Folktales of France,* by Geneviève Massignon, 1968; *Folktales of Germany,* by Kurt Ranke, 1966; *Folktales of Greece,* by Georgios A. Megas, 1977, 1970; *Folktales of Hungary,* by Linda Dégh, 1965; *Folktales of India,* by Brenda E.F. Beck, 1987; *Folktales of Ireland,* by Sean O Súilleabháin, 1966; *Folktales of Israel,* by Dov Noy, 1963; *Folktales of Japan,* by Robert Adams, 1963; *Folktales of Mexico,* by Amérigo Paredes, 1970; *Folktales of Norway,* by Reidar Thoralf Christiansen, 1964; *Folktales Told around the World,* by Richard M. Dorson, 1975.

Fowke, Edith. *Folklore of Canada.* Toronto: McClelland & Stewart, 1976.

Muhawi, Ibrahim, and Sharif Kanaana. *Speak, Bird, Speak Again: Palestinian Arab Folktales.* Berkeley and Los Angeles: Univ. of California Press, 1989.

Simpson, Jacqueline. *Icelandic Folktales and Legends.* Berkeley and Los Angeles: Univ. of California Press, 1972.

Thompson, Stith. *Tales of the North American Indians.* Cambridge, Mass.: Harvard Univ. Press, 1929.

> Includes a valuable bibliography, by tribe, of early collections of Native American tales, many of which were published in journals and government reports.

Vila, Susie Hoogasian. *One Hundred Armenian Tales.* Detroit, Mich.: Wayne State Univ. Press, 1966.

Wilbert, Johannes, and Karin Simoneau. *Folk Literature of South American Indians.* Los Angeles: UCLA Latin American Center Publications, Univ. of California.

> This 23-volume series includes collections of tales of the following tribes. The title of each volume follows the form, *Folk Literature of the* [name of tribe]. All are edited by Wilbert and Simoneau, except as noted. Some are 2-volume sets. *Ayoreo,* 1989; *Bororo,* 1983; *Caduveo,* 1989; *Chamacoco,* 1987; *Chorote,* 1985; *Cuiva,* 1991; *Gê,* 1978, 1984; *Guajiro,* 1985; *Makka,* 1991; *Mataco,* 1982; *Mocoví,* 1988; *Nivaklé,* 1987; *Selknam,* ed. by Martin Gusinde, 1975; *Sikuani,* 1992; *Tehuelche,* 1984; *Toba,* 1982; *Warao,* 1989; *Yamana,* ed. by Martin Gusinde, 1977; *Yanomami,* 1990; and *Yaruro,* 1990.

Studies of tale-types and themes

Many of the following studies include tale summaries along with bibliographic references to source texts. See also the collections on pages 24-25.

Campbell, Joseph. *The Hero with a Thousand Faces.* New York: Pantheon, 1949.

Clodd, Edward. *Tom Tit Tot.* London: Duckworth, 1898.

Texts and summaries of some tales like Rumpelstiltskin.

Clouston, William A. *Popular Tales and Fictions, Their Migrations and Transformations.* 2 vols. Edinburgh: W. Blackwood and Sons, 1887.

Cox, Marian Roalfe. *Cinderella: Three Hundred and Forty-Five Variants of Cinderella, Catskin, and Cap o' Rushes.* London: The Folklore Society, 1893.

Dundes, Alan. *Cinderella: A Casebook.* New York: Garland, 1982.

—. *The Flood Myth.* Berkeley and Los Angeles: Univ. of California Press, 1988.

—. *Little Red Riding Hood: A Casebook.* Madison: Univ. of Wisconsin Press, 1987.

Goldberg, Christine. *Turandot's Sisters: A Study of the Folktale AT 851.* New York: Garland, 1993.

Stories of the riddle princess.

Leavy, Barbara Fass. *In Search of the Swan Maiden: A Narrative on Folklore and Gender.* New York: New York Univ. Press, 1994.

Philip, Neil. *The Cinderella Story.* New York: viking, 1989.

Roberts, Warren E. *The Tale of the Kind and the Unkind Girls: Aa-Th 480 and Related Tales.* Berlin: de Gruyter, 1958.

Rooth, Anna Birgitta. *The Cinderella Cycle.* Lund: Gleerup, 1951.

Swann, Jan Öjvind. *The Tale of Cupid and Psyche.* Lund: Gleerup, 1955.

Finding myths, epics and miscellaneous tale genres

Tale type indexes are used mainly to locate folktales and legends. Motif indexes can be used to find folktales and legends, and also myths from contemporary and recent oral traditions. Finding the sacred texts and epics of vanished civilizations requires a different approach. For one thing, the source texts of these myths are old and often fragmentary. One might imagine that these texts are fixed and unchanging, but that is not the case. New archeological finds can add to our knowledge of a text and even restore a missing part, as happened recently in the case of the Gilgamesh epic. Advancements in scholars' understanding of early Celtic languages has produced translations of Irish and Welsh myth and epic that differ markedly from those of a century ago.

Because of the unique nature of myth and epic texts, a storyteller may want to draw upon the work of skilful retellers, rather than on source material. Children's versions of myths and epics can be located in the volumes of the *Index to Fairy Tales* (see p. 32). The most critically-acclaimed retellings for children are listed in *Children's Catalog* (H.W. Wilson). Adult versions can be located in "best books" bibliographies such as *Public Library Catalog* (H.W. Wilson). Scholars' opinions of the best translations and abridgements of myth and epic can be found in the *Encyclopedia of Religion* (Macmillan, 1987).

For tales of King Arthur and company, see *Index to Fairy Tales* for children's versions, and, for adult material, *The New Arthurian Encyclopedia* (Garland, 1996). Groups of tales that are known by the name of a character such as Robin Hood (from ballads), or Brer Rabbit can be located by character name in the *Index to Fairy Tales* or the *Storyteller's Sourcebook*, and in library catalogs by searching the name of the character as keyword in subject, title, or notes field. The Library of Congress uses some traditional character names as subject headings. The bibliographies of scholarly books and articles about a certain character, tale type, tale genre or storytelling tradition may serve as useful finding aids for tale texts.

CHAPTER FOUR

AROUND & ABOUT
THE TALE

A contemporary storyteller often needs to pursue library research beyond finding tales and variants. The motivation may be to amplify a promising but minimal text, to cast light on some puzzling aspect of a narrative, or simply to find out more about tales and storytelling traditions in other cultures. The recent popularity of the works of Joseph Campbell and other interpreters of folktales has led to the unfortunate belief that anyone can take a tale text from another culture and understand its meaning using intuition and insight. Granted, there are some universal tale themes. Moreover, all oral tales utilize visual imagery, which stimulates meaning-making in readers and listeners, regardless of whether they completely understand the original content and context of the tale or not. However, those who claim Joseph Campbell as their inspiration should realize that he was both a gifted storyteller and a tireless researcher.

It makes sense that a contemporary teller will want to expand, enrich, and even change parts of tales found in books. After all, tales were altered, condensed and impoverished in the process of collection and publication. In addition, traditional storytellers quite naturally omitted background information that was common knowledge to their listeners.

The artistry of the contemporary storyteller who works with traditional material is to make that material meaningful and entertaining to listeners. I don't suggest that research should be done in order to somehow replicate the original tale, or to please folklorists or cultural critics. Rather, I believe that a knowledge of tradition will produce richer, more interesting, more entertaining, and more meaningful tales. A contemporary storyteller can, to some extent, and based on careful research, draw upon the same resources a traditional teller used, changing and updating them, of course, for today's audiences. All tales are part of a tale tradition, which has a common vocabulary of characters, episodes, and textural elements such as songs, chants, traditional openings and closings, etc.

Here is an example of the sort of background research I would contemplate when retelling a tale from a minimal text:

Suppose I find a nursery tale from Ireland called "The Wonderful Cake" that is like "The Gingerbread Boy." The source text is very short, not really enough to make a story. I would like to make it longer by adding some typical Irish storytelling elements, as well as my own creative interpretation. First I would want to see if I could find any variants of the same tale from Ireland. Before consulting *The Types of the Irish Folktale*, I would use *The Types of the Folktale* and the *Motif Index to Folk-Literature* in order to identify the tale types and motifs of the story. The tale is Type 2025, *The Fleeing Pancake*. It is so short that it contains only one motif, Z33.1, "The fleeing pancake." I would then search in two directions, looking for tales of the same tale type in Ireland and in other European cultures, and then looking for other tales of the same genre (formula tales for young children) in Ireland (easier said than done; there is a dearth of nursery tales among the tens of thousands of oral tales collected in Ireland the past hundred years). I would also look for similar tales from Gaelic Scotland, and among tales from North America that might derive from Irish tradition. I would scan animal tales from Ireland to see if I could find traditional ways of describing the hen, the fox, and the other characters in the tale. Because the tale involves a runaway cake, I should investigate traditional Irish cookery. Hmm. I could add a cake-making episode to the tale. This would probably interest young listeners. Perhaps I'll change the word "cake" to an Irish word. I also note that many of the characters in the tale are saying "good day" to each other, and "where are you going?" to the cake. I could find out how to say this in Irish. Maybe I could locate a typical opening and closing formula for the tale as well (though not the formulas used in the Irish hero tales, since that is a different genre entirely, with its own rules of storymaking). Irish friends will be a better and faster resource for finding these bits of language than books. And I can't forget visual details. I'd want descriptions, drawings or photographs of rural Irish houses and villages (I've travelled in Ireland, so some of this resides in my memory). All of this research would send me to many parts of both the public and university library, and to friends and acquaintances as well. Along the way I might have to give up some of my ideas, and I will certainly think of others.

Tale research leads in many directions. The better you know your basic reference sources, such as the tale type indexes and tale collections from your areas of interest, the easier your task will be. Depending upon your research topic and goals, you will need to use tale type and motif indexes, search library catalogs and periodical indexes, and browse the introductions, contents, notes and bibliographies of scholarly works. The following is a guide to the best library resources around and about traditional tales:

Basic reference guides

When you haven't got a clue where to look for information, it's wisest to begin your search with the standard library bibliographies, compiled by experts, rather than browsing a library's shelves or catalog. These two books will refer you to the most authoritative and up-to-date bibliographies, encyclopedias, and dictionaries on every subject imaginable:

Balay, Robert, ed. *Guide to Reference Books*. 11th ed. Chicago: American Library Association, 1996.

Day, Alan, and Joan M. Harvey. *Walford's Guide to Reference Material*. London: Library Association Publishing, 1995.

Folklore and anthropology bibliographies:

Steinfirst, Susan. *Folklore and Folklife: A Guide to English Language Reference Sources*. 2 vols. New York: Garland, 1992.

> A comprehensive, well-annotated bibliography of the best resources for finding out about all types of folklore in all parts of the world.

Weeks, John M. *Introduction to Library Research in Anthropology*. Boulder, Co.: Westview Press, 1991.

Westerman, R.C. *Fieldwork in the Library: A Guide to Research in Anthropology and Related Area Studies*. Chicago: American Library Association, 1994.

> These two works will direct you to country and area bibliographies, which in turn will lead you to sources of information on your subject.

Indexes to books and articles

Dissertations Abstracts International. University Microfilms, 1861-

> This entire database is available on CD-ROM and through various online services, and includes keyword-searchable abstracts for dissertations published since 1980. Dissertations can be excellent sources of bibliographies on obscure topics. Libraries will not ordinarily send bound volumes on interlibrary loan (the binding is fragile) but may lend microfilm copies.

Humanities Index. H.W. Wilson, 1974- (previously part of the *Social Sciences and Humanities Index*, 1916-1974).

An index to U.S. journals and magazines.

Internationale Volkskundliche Bibliographie/International Folklore and Folklife Bibliography/Bibliographie internationale des arts et traditions populaires. Basel: G. Krebs, 1917-

> A multilingual international index to folklore articles. The *IVB* has a subject index in English.

MLA International Bibliography of Books and Articles on the Modern Languages and Literatures. Modern Language Association of America, 1921-

> With the *Internationale Volkskundliche Bibliographie* (above), the *MLA Bibliography* provides the most complete indexing of folklore, including journals, serials, books, essays in collections, conference papers and dissertations. Indexing since 1963 is available on CD-rom and online.

Social Sciences Index. H.W. Wilson, 1974- (continues the *Social Sciences and Humanities Index,* 1916-1974).

An index to articles in U.S. journals and magazines.

Journals and magazines

Early publications of folklore societies, such as the *Journal of American Folklore* and the British journal *Folklore* are filled with tale texts and articles about oral narrative. In the 1960s, the direction of folklore studies changed radically, particularly in the U.S. Scholarly activity shifted from the collection of texts and the study of traditional narrative genres to analysis of folklore performance the development of theory. Texts and studies of folktales, myth, legend and epic are published in a wide range of scholarly journals outside folklore. If you want to keep up-to-date in a particular area, it's best to do frequent subject searches of electronic periodical indexes such as the *MLA Bibliography,* rather than trying to browse through every likely journal in the library. When you find a journal that is of continuing interest to you, you can scan the table of contents of the latest issues via

ContentsFirst, available online and updated daily. Ask a librarian about access.

Only a few academic journals specialize in oral traditional tales and storytelling. The most important is the trilingual *Fabula: Revue d'études sur le conte populaire/Zeitschrift für Erzählforschung/ Journal of Folktale Studies* (Berlin, Germany: Walter de Gruyter, 1958-). Scholars from many countries publish articles in English in *Fabula,* and it is an excellent source of well-researched, well-documented articles. *Merveilles & Contes/ Marvels & Tales/Wunder & Märchen/ Maravillas & Cuentos/ Meraviglie & Racconti* (Univ. of Colorado, 1987-) publishes articles about fairy tales and fantasy from both the oral and literary traditions. The quality of the articles is uneven, but some top-notch writers contribute. Another important academic journal, entirely in French, is *Cahiers de littérature orale.*

Parabola: The Magazine of Myth and Tradition (New York: Society for the Study of Myth and Tradition, 1976-) is a magazine about "the quest for meaning." In addition to articles, *Parabola* publishes several literary retellings of traditional tales in each issue. It is a good source of book reviews (the academic journals are dismally slow in reviewing new books). *Storytelling Magazine* (Jonesboro, Tenn.: National Storytelling Association, 1984-), the trade journal of contemporary U.S. storytellers, publishes how-to articles, tale texts and book reviews. The folklore expertise of contributing writers varies.

Folklore journals, including many national and regional publications, can be located using *Ulrich's International Periodical Directory,* published by R.R. Bowker. The entries in *Ulrich's* are organized by subject. Individual entries contain information about the periodical, including where each one is indexed, and which document delivery services will furnish photocopies of articles.

Cultural resources

In order to understand the realistic aspects of tales, a researcher will want to seek out studies of the lives of ordinary people, rather than official history. In academia, the term *everyday life* is used for studies of urban folks, *folklife* for studies of rural and peasant classes, and *ethnology* for studies of nonwestern people. Everyday life is usually the province of historians, folklife of folklorists, and ethnology of anthropologists. Works about the traditions of specific countries can be located in catalogs and indexes by searching the name of the region, country, ethnic group, or culture + keywords such as ethnology, ethnography, anthropology, folklife, customs, and everyday life. LC subject headings are Ethnology, Anthropology, Social life and customs, and Social history. The following sources are good beginning points for research into a culture. Bear in mind that the names of tribal and ethnic groups may have changed over the years.

Levinson, David, ed. *Encyclopedia of World Cultures.* 10 vols. Boston, Mass.: G.K. Hall, 1991-96.

> This is a good place to look first for information about an ethnic group, such as its geographical location, customs, and language, and for bibliographies.

Carlisle, Richard, ed. *Illustrated Encyclopedia of Mankind.* 22 vols. Marshall Cavendish, 1990.

> Organized by ethnic group and well-indexed, this reference set is less scholarly than the *Encyclopedia of World Cultures.* It is illustrated with many color photographs.

National Geographic Index 1888-1988. National Geographic Society, 1989.

Tale traditions

The best single source of articles and bibliographies about traditional tales and storytelling is the German *Enzyklopädie des Märchens,* a multivolume work that is still in process (over half of the volumes have been published). National and regional tale traditions are seldom the subject of book-length studies. In English, works about European, North American, Native North

American, and sub-Saharan African narrative are by far the most plentiful. Chapters on oral tradition are often included in general books on the literature of a country or language. The study of oral narrative is accorded more importance, generally, in countries and cultures where written language and literature are fairly recent. Other good sources of information about tale traditions are the introductions and notes in tale anthologies, and in tale type and motif indexes. Also consult the bibliogrpahies of these works. Journal articles, books, dissertations, essays in collections and conference papers on the subject can be located in the *MLA Bibliography.*

To locate books and articles in library catalogs and indexes, use the name of the country, region, ethnic group or culture + keywords such as folktales, legends, myths, mythology, oral literature, folk literature, oral tradition, oral narrative, folk narrative. Library of Congress subject headings are Folklore, Tales, Legends, Myths, Mythology, Folk literature, and Oral tradition.

General reference works

Bennett, Gillian. *Contemporary Legend: A Folklore Bibliography.* New York: Garland, 1993.

Bonnefoy, Yves, ed. *Mythologies.* 2 vols. Chicago: Univ. of Chicago Press, 1991.

> This very comprehensive scholarly work has also been issued in three abridged volumes, all published by the University of Chicago Press: *American, African, and Old European Mythologies* (1993), *Greek and Egyptian Mythologies* (1992) and *Roman and European Mythologies* (1992).

Carnes, Pack. *Fable Scholarship: An Annotated Bibliography.* New York: Garland, 1985.

Eliade, Mircea, ed. *The Encyclopedia of Religion.* 16 vols. Macmillan, 1987. Also available in CD-ROM format.

> Contains very readable scholarly articles on myth and epic.

Enzyklopädie des Märchens, ed. by Kurt Ranke, *et. al.* Berlin: de Gruyter, 1975-

> This encyclopedia of tales is (or will be when completed) the most extensive, authoritative work about the oral narrative tradition. Each of the twelve volumes is issued in five parts, currently volume 8 is in process. The bibliographies are mammoth and multilingual; for example, the bibliography of works about Nasruddin Hodja is six pages long, in fine print. If the first letter of the German word for your topic is in the first half of the alphabet, by all means consult this encyclopedia, which includes articles about tale types, genres, characters, themes, and national and regional oral narrative traditions.

Grimal, Pierre, ed. *Larousse World Mythology.* Hamlyn, 1965.

Leach, Maria, ed. *Funk and Wagnalls Standard Dictionary of Folklore, Mythology, and Legend.* San Francisco: Harper and Row, 1984.

> Though only slightly updated from the 1948-9 edition, this remains a useful reference source for folklore and mythology. More like an encyclopedia than a dictionary, it includes both long articles and short entries.

Mercatante, Anthony S., ed. *Facts on File Encyclopedia of World Mythology and Legend.* New York: Facts on File, 1988.

New Larousse Encyclopedia of Myth. Putnam, 1968.

Thompson, Stith. *The Folktale.* New York: Holt, Rinehart & Winston, 1948.

> Outdated in its concepts of other cultures "borrowing" tales from the Indo-European cultures, and its labeling of cultures as "primitive," this book is nonetheless helpful in understanding the Aarne-Thompson classification system of tale types. Contains a valuable bibliography, by culture, of the major tale collections published 1812-1945.

Europe

Baer, Florence E. *Folklore and Literature of the British Isles: An Annotated Bibliography*. New York: Garland, 1986.

Falassi, Alessandro. *Italian Folklore: An Annotated Bibliography*. New York: Garland, 1985.

Holbek, Bengt. *Interpretation of Fairy Tales*. Folklore Fellows Communications 239. Helsinki: Suomalainen Tiedeakatemia, 1987.

> Enroute to interpreting some Danish fairy tales, Holbek provides an excellent overview of folktale studies in Europe, and of the various methods of analysis, from psychoanalytical to structural, that have been applied to them.

Lüthi, Max. *The European Folktale: Form and Nature*. Philadelphia: Institute for the Study of Human Issues, 1982.

—. *The Fairy Tale as Art Form and Portrait of Man*. Bloomington: Indiana Univ. Press, 1984.

Miller, Julia E. *Modern Greek Folklore: An Annotated Bibliography*. New York: Garland, 1985.

Oinas, Felix J. *Heroic Epic and Saga*. Bloomington: Indiana Univ. Press, 1978.

Propp, Vladimir. *Morphology of the Folktale*. 2nd ed. Austin: Univ. of Texas Press, 1968.

> Propp intended to devise a classification system for Russian fairy tales, but instead came to the conclusion that all fairy tales share the same basic plot.

Ward, Donald. *The German Legends of the Brothers Grimm*. 2 vols. Philadelphia: Institute for the Study of Human Issues, 1981.

> A lesser known Grimm collection. The essay and comparative notes provide valuable information about supernatural, historical and local legends.

The Americas

Bierhorst, John. *The Mythology of Mexico and Central America.* New York: Morrow, 1990.

—. *The Mythology of North America.* New York: Morrow, 1985.

—. *The Mythology of South America.* New York: Morrow, 1988.

Brown, Carolyn S. *The Tall Tale in American Folklore and Literature.* Knoxville: Univ. of Tennessee Press, 1987.

Brunvand, Jan, ed. *American Folklore: An Encyclopedia.* New York: Garland, 1996.

Clements, William M. *Native American Folklore, 1879-1979: An Annotated Bibliography.* Athens, Ohio: Swallow Press, 1984.

Fowke, Edith F. *A Bibliography of Canadian Folklore in English.* Toronto: Univ. of Toronto Press, 1981.

Georges, Robert, and Stephen Stern. *American and Canadian Immigrant and Ethnic Folklore: An Annotated Bibliography.* New York: Garland, 1982.

Haywood, Charles. *A Bibliography of North American Folklore and Folksong.* 2 vols. 2nd rev. ed. New York: Dover, 1961.

Heisley, Michael. *An Annotated Bibliography of Chicano Folklore from the Southwestern United States.* Los Angeles: Center for the Study of Comparative Folklore and Mythology, UCLA, 1977.

MacGregor-Villarreal, Mary. *Brazilian Folk Narrative Scholarship: A Critical Survey and Selective Annotated Bibliography.* New York: Garland, 1994.

Niles, Susan A. *South American Indian Narrative, Theoretical and Analytical Approaches: An Annotated Bibliography.* New York: Garland, 1981.

Szwed, John F. *Afro-American Folk Culture: An Annotated Bibliography of Materials for North, Central, and South America, and the West Indies.* Philadelphia: Institute for the Study of Human Issues, 1978.

Wiget, Andrew, ed. *Dictionary of Native American Literature.* New York: Garland, 1994.

Yassif, Eli. *Jewish Folklore: An Annotated Bibliography.* New York: Garland, 1986.

Africa and the Middle East

Avakian, Anne M. *Armenian Folklore Bibliography.* Berkeley and Los Angeles: Univ. of California Press, 1994.

Coughlan, Margaret N. *Folklore from Africa to the United States: An Annotated Bibliography.* Washington: Library of Congress, 1976.

Okpewho, Isidore. *African Oral Literature: Backgrounds, Character and Continuity.* Bloomington: Indiana Univ. Press, 1992.

Radhayrapetian, Juliet. *Iranian Folk Narrative: A Survey of Scholarship.* New York: Garland, 1990.

Scheub, Harold. *African Oral Narratives, Proverbs, Riddles, Poetry, and Song.* Boston: G.K. Hall, 1977.

An annotated bibliography.

Asia

Algarin, Joanne P. *Japanese Folk Literature: A Core Collection and Reference Guide.* New York: R.R. Bowker, 1983.

Bernardo, Gabriel Adriano. *A Critical and Annotated Bibliography of Philippine, Indonesian and other Malayan Folk-Lore.* Cagayan de Oro City, Philippines: Xavier Univ., 1972.

Handoo, Jawaharlal. *A Bibliography of Indian Folk Literature.* Mysore: Central Institute of Indian Languages, 1977.

Kirkland, Edwin Capers. *A Bibliography of South Asian Folklore.* Bloomington: Indiana Univ. Research Center in Anthropology, Folklore, and Linguistics, 1966.

Ting, Nai-Tung. *Chinese Folk Narratives: A Bibliographical Guide.* San Francisco: Chinese Materials Center, 1975.

Australia and Pacific Islands

Davey, Gwenda, and Graham Seal, eds. *The Oxford Companion to Australian Folklore.* Melbourne: Oxford University Press, 1993.

Haynes, Douglas E. *Micronesian Religion and Lore: A Guide to Sources, 1526-1990.* Westport, Conn.: Greenwood Press, 1995.

Leib, Amos P., and A. Grove Day. *Hawaiian Legends in English: An Annotated Bibliography.* 2nd ed. Honolulu: Univ. Press of Hawaii, 1975.

Orbell, Margaret Rose. *A Select Bibliography of the Oral Tradition of Oceania.* Auckland, N.Z.: University of Auckland, 1975.

Folk belief

The magical and supernatural elements in tales from the oral tradition are more likely to reflect folk belief systems than the dogma of official religion. For example, the most useful belief material for understanding the magic in European fairy tales is what Jacob and Wilhelm Grimm termed "lower mythology." The creatures of this lower mythology were quite literally lower than the Greek or Norse gods, since they dwelled beneath the earth or underwater. The older belief systems of Europe live on in the fairy tales, legends and superstitions of Europeans and European Americans. Works about superstitions can be useful in puzzling out details of folktales and legends.

Resources for learning more about folk beliefs are scattered among several academic disciplines and library subject areas. The closest LC subject headings are Religion, Superstition, and the intriguing "Medicine, Magic, Mystic & Spargic." Try title

keyword searches using the terms folk belief, folk religion, traditional religion + the name of the region, country, ethnic group
or culture. A good folklore or anthropology bibliography for the
specific culture you are researching should also be useful.

Bächtold-Stäuble, Hanns, ed. *Handwörterbuch des deutschen
Aberglaubens.* 10 vols. Berlin: W. de Gruyter, 1927-1942.

> The grandmother of folk belief collections, with compara-
> tive notes and references to beliefs worldwide. Some biblio-
> graphic citations are to works in English.

Cavendish, Richard, and Brian Innes, eds. *Man, Myth and
Magic: The Illustrated History of Mythology, Religion and the
Unknown.* New ed. 21 vols. New York: Marshall Cavendish,
1995.

> This work covers a wide range of beliefs, from religion to
> magic and the occult, though none in great depth. Many
> color illustrations.

Eliade, Mircea, ed. *Encyclopedia of Religion.* 16 vols. New York:
Macmillan, 1986. Also available on CD-ROM.

> An excellent source of information and bibliographies on
> nontraditional religions and beliefs, as well as more estab-
> lished ones.

Hastings, James, ed. *Encyclopedia of Religion and Ethics.* 13
vols. Edinburgh: T. and T. Clark, 1908-26.

> The most knowledgeable scholars of the time contributed to
> this encyclopedia, and nonwestern cultures are well-repre-
> sented among the articles (be sure to search using circa-1900
> country names).

Frazer, James. *The Golden Bough: A Study in Magic and Religion.*
3rd ed. 12 vols. London: Macmillan, 1907-15.

> An extensive, well-indexed compilation of beliefs and rituals,
> useful even if Frazer's theories are dated.

Hand, Wayland D. *Popular Beliefs and Superstitions from North Carolina*. Frank C. Brown Collection of North Carolina Folklore, vols. 6 and 7. Durham, N.C.: Duke Univ. Press, 1961.

> A classified collection of Appalachian beliefs, with comparative notes and references to related material from other areas.

Opie, Iona, and Moira Tatem, eds. *Dictionary of Superstitions*. Oxford: Oxford Univ. Press, 1989.

> Superstitions from the British Isles.

Puckett, Newbell Niles. *Popular Beliefs and Superstitions: A Compendium of American Folklore from the Ohio Collection of Newbell Niles Puckett*. 3 vols. Boston, Mass.: G.K. Hall, 1981.

> Includes beliefs and superstitions from a broad range of U.S. ethnic groups.

Oral style

Tales in books are not likely to reflect the oral performance style of the those who once told them. Texts are likely to have been condensed into a synopsis or outline form, or rewritten as literary short stories. With some exceptions (such as the anthologies listed in *Chapter 2:Tellable Tales*) book tales must be resuscitated for oral telling. A contemporary teller often has a signature style for adapting a tale for performance; however, it can be useful as well to investigate how a tale was told in its place of origin. Of course, the way in which a tale was told in another time and location might be inappropriate for a contemporary audience. Modern audiences have expectations of entertainers that a storyteller ignores at her own peril. Traditional storytelling styles run the gamut from dynamic call-and-response style from parts of Africa, to the very subdued recitation of many Irish tellers of wonder tales. Stylistic elements that can be integrated into a modern telling include traditional openings and closings, songs and chants, and onomatopoeia. Traditional openings and closings are included in some tale anthologies, and also in Anne Pellowski's *World of Storytelling* (H.W. Wilson,

1991). Bilingual tale anthologies can be a good source of chants, songs, onomatopoeia, native language names for characters, etc. A few anthologists include native language storytelling vocbulary in English translations, as Robert Adams did in *Folktales of Japan* and "Social Identity of a Japanese Storyteller." Traditional storytellers and others familiar with storytelling in a particular culture, are invaluable resources.

The following are important works in the field of oral style:

Lord, Albert Bates. *The Singer of Tales.* Cambridge: Harvard Univ. Press, 1960.

> Albert Lord and Milman Parry studied the traditional epic singers of Yugoslavia in order to demonstrate that the *Iliad* and *Odyssey* were probably composed orally.

Ong, Walter. *Orality and Literacy: The Technologizing of the Word.* New York: Methuen, 1982.

> Ong attempted to demonstrate the profound ways in which the nonliterate mind differs from the literate. Ong's work, along with that of Albert Lord, helped create the academic field of oral-formulaic studies.

Tedlock, Dennis. *The Spoken Word and the Work of Interpretation.* Philadelphia: Univ. of Pennsylvania Press, 1983.

> Tedlock pioneered methods of representing oral style in the typography of a text, using the placement of words on the page, typeface and type size to give the reader a better sense of tales in performance.

Storytelling traditions

Most early collections of oral narrative presented texts while ignoring the tellers, since scholars believed that traditional storytellers merely repeated tales verbatim. Since the 1930s, however, the creativity of traditional storytellers has been recognized by fieldworkers, with support from theorists. The following list includes some of the most important and readable works on the

subject. For references to other accounts of traditional storytellers and storytelling, consult Ellin Greene and George
Shannon's *Storytelling: A Selected Annotated Bibliography* (New
York : Garland, 1986) and Anne Pellowski's *World of Storytelling* (Bronx, N.Y.: H.W. Wilson, 1990), which includes an
excellent, extensive bibliography. To locate other works on the
subject, search using Storytellers, Storytelling, and Oral tradition as either keywords or LC subject headings + the name of
the country, region, ethnic group or culture.

Adams, Robert J. "Social Identity of a Japanese Storyteller." 2
vols. Ph.D. diss. Indiana Univ., 1972.

> The tales and life of a Japanese farming woman who taught
> herself to read in middle age in order to add more stories to
> her repertoire.

Cosentino, Donald. *Defiant Maids and Stubborn Farmers:
Tradition and Innovation in Mende Story Performance.*
Cambridge: Cambridge Univ. Press, 1982.

> This book opens with a competition between three story-
> tellers, who relate very different versions of the same tale.

Crowley, Daniel. *I Could Talk Old-Story Good: Creativity in
Bahamian Folklore.* Berkeley and Los Angeles: Univ. of
California Press, 1966.

> A detailed study of how storytelling functioned in a small
> island community.

Dégh, Linda. *Folktales and Society: Story-Telling in a Hungarian
Peasant Community.* Revised ed. Bloomington: Indiana Univ.
Press, 1989.

> Linda Dégh studied traditional narrators over many years
> and documented how changing status, including national
> recognition and honors, affected the lives and repertoires of
> the tellers.

——. *Narratives in Society: A Performer-Centered Study of Narration.* Folklore Fellows Communications 255. Helsinki: Suomalainen Tiedeakatemia, 1995.

A collection of essays by one of the world's leading tale scholars. Includes an English-language translation of Dégh's article "The Nature of Women's Storytelling" from the *Enzyklopädie des Märchens.*

Falassi, Alessandro. *Folklore by the Fireside: Text and Context of the Tuscan Veglia.* Austin: Univ. of Texas Press, 1980.

Falassi describes how familiar European tales were told in Italian homes in the not-too-distant past.

Scheub, Harold. *Xhosa Ntsomi.* Oxford: Clarendon Press, 1975.

The texts of South African call-and-response tales, along with an exploration of how storytellers improvised tales in performance.

Zenani, Nongenile Masitha. *The Word and the World: Tales and Observations from the Xhosa Oral Tradition.* Edited by Harold Scheub. Madison: Univ. of Wisconsin Press, 1992.

This work combines tale texts with autobiography and tale interpretation by the storyteller herself.

CHAPTER FIVE

FIELDWORK

Fieldwork is research based on observation and interviews outside the laboratory or library. I find the word especially appropriate, for just as a farmer can't simply go out into a field and find a crop there, waiting, ready for the harvest, so a fieldworker can't simply go out, tape recorder in hand, and find tales. Cultural fieldwork requires library research, careful preparation, and most of all, developing relationships with the people one intends to interview or observe. I have conducted most of my own fieldwork among contemporary storytellers and their audiences, and I have learned an enormous amount from them. I have also worked with storytellers and story-knowers from other cultures. In some cases, people have spontaneously shared stories and information about storytelling, and my main concern was recording it quickly and accurately. In other cases, I have sought out information and stories from cultural experts. This work has been very rewarding but also extremely challenging and demanding. It requires background research, tact, perseverance, follow-up and often the assistance of translators.

How and why would a contemporary storyteller conduct fieldwork? A storyteller might well imagine that he will find and record complete tales that audiences would want to hear or read. While this certainly could happen, there are many other ways a teller can benefit from interviewing and consulting with people who have a knowledge of tales and storytelling. Information other than complete tales can be interesting and useful to a storyteller. A recollection of how a person imagined Anansi, or Jack, or Coyote, or of the feelings elicited by a ghost story, or a description of where and how stories are or were told can help a contemporary storyteller shape tales, and can also be shared with audiences. Cultural experts can help a contemporary storyteller determine whether a tale and tale elements are traditional in a certain region or among a certain group of people, help translate a tale text and share bits of storytelling vocabulary such as traditional openings and closings.

Opportunities to record story-related information can come at any time. For this reason, it is a good idea to carry a small notebook dedicated solely to storytelling (this can be the same notebook you use for library research). Don't trust your memory! You are as likely to mis-remember important ideas, words and phrases as you are to forget them. In a study on memory for folktales, psychologist F. C. Bartlett found that his research subjects were most certain about the parts of stories they remembered incorrectly.

In your public role as storyteller, you will be approached by people wanting to share tales, or anecdotes about storytelling, but it's a good idea also to actively seek such information. Those who know the most may be too shy to speak up. Richard Dorson, who trained many of America's most eminent folklorists, recommended that beginning fieldworkers gather lore from members of their own families. This can be good practice in the art and technique of interviewing, and can also furnish details of family and local history that can be woven into personal experience stories.

Where to find stories

There are some common misconceptions about who knows stories: *only* people from exotic cultures know stories, *all* people from exotic cultures know stories, *only* elders know stories, or *all* elders know stories. There are many people who think that traditional storytelling is dead. While it's true that there is much less now than in the days before inexpensive books, films, radio, and the ubiquitous television, there are many people who still tell tales, who once told tales, or who have memories of storytelling. Studies have shown how easily tale traditions can be revived, and published tale texts have played a crucial role in this process. See for example the article by Kay Stone, cited in the bibliography at the end of this chapter.

"To know stories" is a phrase that can describe a wide range of remembered knowledge and storytelling proficiency, from a polished performer who can tell stories at the drop of a hat, to someone who can only haltingly recall the bare bones of a tale heard but never told. As I read older tale collections, I suspect that many texts were gathered from the latter type of person. Even in the case of a skilled storyteller, there is an enormous difference between recounting the plot of a tale to a stranger who does not understand one's language well, and bringing it to life before a receptive audience. This does not, of course, mean that plot summaries or awkward retellings don't have value; however they are valuable only in conjunction with other, related data.

Young people can be quite accomplished storytellers, especially if they have had good adult models. Some children as young as four will often recite a favorite story down to the tiniest detail, even reproducing vocal inflection and gestures, though the ability to change and improvise a tale for an audience comes several years later. Most elementary-age children are able to remember and recount tale plots. Sometimes a young person's storytelling ability can be too good, as in a case reported by Canadian folklorist Vivian Labrie. She was collecting fairy tales from a French Canadian couple, and their son arrived during a recording session. He said that he knew a male Cinderella story, and began telling it. Labrie was understandably delighted, until she realized that he was telling the plot of the Jerry Lewis film *Cinderfella*. ("Cendrillon aux grands pieds." *Cahiers de littérature orale* 25 [1989]). If you collect stories from children, be aware that you will hear book tales that are not necessarily traditional in the child's culture. There are even documented cases of traditional storytellers who, wishing to add to their repertoire in order to please their local audience or a tale collector, learned and retold tales from books. When children tell you stories, be sensitive to attitudes toward traditional tales in their families, and do not record or retell tales you hear from children unless you discuss it with their parents.

Adult memory poses a different sort of problem for a fieldworker. Often, those who once knew tales well, as listeners or as tellers, can't recall them well enough years later to recount them to a fieldworker. Yet once people have a reason to remember, they begin to reconstruct the tales in their memories. The process may require days or even weeks, and the fieldworker will need to stay in contact with the person, and offer encouragement.

When a contemporary storyteller tells tales, listeners are often prompted to respond in kind. In some cultures, it's a socially-required exchange. When I taught storytelling workshops to teachers in Los Angeles, I heard stories from many of the participants, especially those who were recent immigrants. There were two components of those workshops which I believe led people to tell me so many stories. First, I would begin each session by telling folktales that have many international variants, mostly animals tales and formula tales. This seemed to prime their memories for similar tales they knew. Second, we spent a good part of each workshop making feltboard figures, and this created a friendly atmosphere in which sharing tales was natural and non-threatening.

Interviewing

Fieldwork can be done informally and recorded by means of written notes, but there will be times when you believe someone has a store of knowledge that will be interesting to you, to other storytellers, and to audiences. In these cases, you will want to schedule a formal interview, do some background research, and record your conversation on audiotape or video. When you do this, you will be entering into a special relationship with the person you interview. Don't ever work with someone you don't like or don't trust, or who has unrealistic expectations of what you will do with the information—such as publish a book and make him rich and famous. The best storytelling fieldwork is accomplished between people who consider themselves equals, and who share a love and respect for tales and storytelling. Be sure you inform the interviewee how you plan to use the knowledge he is sharing with you.

Before the interview, you will want to research the storytelling traditions the person is most likely to know. Inquire about his ethnic background, where he lived as a child, where his parents grew up, and what languages were spoken in the home. You can use these terms to guide your library search. If you can't find material about his exact group or place of origin, search for information about nearby areas with related cultures. A brief list of the names of typical tale characters, plot synopses, etc., may be very useful in stimulating an interviewee's memory. Your research will also help you to develop questions during the course of the interview.

Equipment

It was difficult for me to begin using a tape recorder in fieldwork, but now I can't recommend it strongly enough. Whether they are telling tales or sharing information about tales, people will use words unfamiliar to you, and even chant rhymes, or sing songs. In most interview situations, audiotaping is probably preferable to videotaping, which may intimidate the interviewee, and requires a camera operator. Of course, videotaping or photographing will be necessary if a person is sharing visual information, such as string figures. I don't ask in advance if I can audiotape an interview. I arrange to interview the person at a table, and simply set up the recorder and remark casually that I'll be recording the interview. If the person expresses concern, I explain that his knowledge is very important, and that I can't possibly write down or remember all he says. I assure him that I will not play the tape for anyone else without permission. If he still objects, of course, I do not tape the interview. I find that most people don't mind, and even those who are nervous initially soon forget the tape recorder. I use either a recorder with built-in microphone or a small personal recorder with a separate microphone. I set the recorder on a tabletop, halfway between us, on a cushion of foam (in case the table is jostled). I use a tape that has 45 minutes per side, and I don't start the tape recorder until the actual interview begins, in order to minimize the need to change the tape. Before the interview, I label the tape with the date and subject, and speak the same information into the microphone.

When I took a folklore fieldwork course in graduate school, I never had the opportunity to observe an experienced fieldworker in action. I had, however, been interviewed by newspaper reporters, and I decided to model my technique on theirs. I try to be organized and neat, friendly yet businesslike. Most people living and working in the U.S. can relate well to this style, but when interviewing people of an unfamiliar culture and language, it may be necessary to work with a translator or with a bicultural assistant.

I create a list of questions I want to ask in an interview. I may or may not ask all of them, and will certainly think of more, but I can always fall back on the list. I make no attempt to hide the list of questions or my notes from the interviewee. I believe that people share information with me during a formal interview that they wouldn't share during a simple conversation. The situation evokes a sense of history that leads people to remember long-forgotten events, and to have new insights. I have even found this to be true when I have interviewed close friends.

Often, the people I am interviewing will tell me a story, but seldom will anyone tell a story in the same way they would to their usual audience. In order to observe a performance of a tale, a fieldworker will either have to happen upon a storytelling session, or arrange for one to happen. An arranged session must replicate the sort of occasion in which the person would ordinarily tell a story. Facing a seated audience in a well-lit room is not a typical storytelling environment in most cultures! It may require more than one taping session for the teller and audience to become accustomed to your presence.

I've found it is crucial that I listen to audiotapes and type up my notes as soon as possible after a recording session. Not only is it easier for me to decipher the tape immediately afterward, but nearly always there will be points I need to clarify with the interviewee. Transcribing word for word from a tape is a tedious and sometimes frustrating process. Unlike an academic folklorist, a storyteller probably won't require an exact transcription of every bit of a recording session, but will simply write a summary, with certain parts transcribed exactly.

Recommended reading

Fine, Elizabeth C. *The Folklore Text: From Performance to Print.* Bloomington: Indiana Univ. Press, 1984.

> A very academic overview of the history and theory of creating texts from oral performance.

Georges, Robert A., and Michael Owen Jones. *People Studying People: The Human Element in Fieldwork.* Berkeley and Los Angeles: Univ. of California Press, 1980.

> This fascinating exposé of the darker (and lighter) side of folklore and anthropology helps a researcher prepare realistically for fieldwork.

Stone, Kay. "Old Stories, New Listeners." In *Who Says? Essays on Pivotal Issues in Contemporary Storytelling*, edited by Carol L. Birch and Melissa A. Heckler. Little Rock, Ark.: August House Publishers, 1996.

> An account of the unique collaboration, as writers and performers, between the Canadian Gaelic-language storyteller Joe Neil MacNeil and field researcher John Shaw.

Walker, Barbara K. "The Folks Who Tell Folk Tales: Field Collecting in Turkey." *Horn Book* 47:6 (December 1971): 636-42.

Walker explains how she collected folktales, translated them, and adapted them for children.

Wolkstein, Diane. *The Magic Orange Tree and Other Haitian Folk Tales.* New York: Knopf, 1978.

In her introduction and tale notes, Wolkstein describe the storytellers and the circumstances in which she collected these dramatic tales.

CHAPTER SIX

COPYRIGHT
FOR STORYTELLERS

Do you need to worry about copyright laws? Unless you are a teacher telling stories within your school, or a librarian performing in your library, or a minister using tales in religious services, the answer is probably yes. When you read or hear a tale you want to tell, you need to determine if it is copyrighted. If it is, you may need to obtain permission from the copyright owner in order to use it.

First the disclaimer: I am not a lawyer. I have had to educate myself on the subject of copyright over the past fifteen years, first as a children's entertainer, then as a compiler of folktale anthologies. My research into copyright laws was aided by attorney Janet L. Gupton's master's thesis, "An examination of copyright laws as applied to the realm of theatre artists" (University of Oregon, 1993). The information that follows is a general overview of copyright law as it relates to storytellers.

Some storytellers are too cautious about copyright, requesting permission to use tales that are actually in the public domain, and can be used freely by anyone. Others declare themselves not interested in copyright. Copyright is the law of the land, and storytellers need to know how it affects them. Copyright laws and the self-help books about copyright will not provide unambiguous answers to every question about what material may and may not be used without permission of the copyright owner. In the end each storyteller must make the best and most informed decision possible. While the law provides penalties for copyright infringement, any disputes that may arise between a storyteller who has unintentionally violated copyright and a copyright owner could probably be settled amicably with the payment of a small permission fee.

Every storyteller should read relevant portions of at least one up-to-date book on the subject of copyright written by an attorney or other expert. Teachers, librarians, and others who tell stories as a part of their jobs in nonprofit educational institutions will want to read *The Copyright Primer for Librarians and Educators,* by Janis Bruwelheide (American Library Association, 1995). Other storytellers can benefit from copyright handbooks published for writers. Writers, like storytellers, often use and adapt the works of others, and need to know which texts can be copied or adapted fairly, and which require permission from the copyright owner. Copyright manuals for writers also explain how to protect one's own creations through copyright, a subject that should be of interest to professional storytellers. The best book I have found of this sort is *The Copyright Handbook: How to Protect and Use Written Works,* by Stephen Fishman (Berkeley, Ca.: Nolo Press, 1996). It is also possible, of course, to consult an attorney who specializes in copyright. The Library of Congress Copyright Office has a home page on the World Wide Web (http://lcweb.loc.gov/copyright/) that provides the text of sections of the copyright law and the full texts of Copyright Office publications.

Revisions in U.S. copyright law are likely to occur soon in order to better define how copyright applies to electronic media. Also, bills extending the length of copyright protection have been introduced in Congress. The magazine or newspaper index at your local library will help you keep abreast of the latest articles on the subject. Nolo Press furnishes copyright updates on the World Wide Web at http://www.nolo.com/intprop.html.

It is not a good idea to get your information about copyright from other storytellers unless you are confident that they have thoroughly researched the subject. I have observed that tellers tend to invent justifications not to heed copyright law, such as "I don't need to worry about copyright because I'm not charging any money," "No one can copyright a folktale," or "I can use a tale if I find it in two different books, or if I retell it using different words." Each of these arguments could lead to violation of copyright law.

What is copyright?

Article I, Section 8 of the United States Constitution provides that "The Congress shall have the power . . . To promote the Progress of Science and the useful Arts, by securing for limited Times to Authors and Inventors the exclusive Right to their respective Writings and Discoveries." A primary goal of copyright law is to encourage the creation of new works by assuring that the creators of the works can profit from them. Copyright is the right, protected by law, to own one's artistic creations and to control what others do with them. The term 'artistic' is used quite loosely; only a minimal amount of creativity is required in order for a work to be copyrightable. Copyright is actually a bundle of rights, giving the owner control over reproduction of the work in various media, by various means, and over works derived from the work (such as a movie made from a novel). Copyright does not last forever. After a certain amount of time (depending upon when and in what country a work was first created), a work enters the public domain and may be freely copied by anyone. If an author or artist adapts or expands an existing work, he can copyright his contribution to the work, but not the underlying work itself (and must obtain permission to adapt a copyrighted work). In addition, facts and ideas may not be copyrighted.

The legal rights of the creator of the work include control over its public performance. To perform a work is defined in the Copyright Act as "to recite, render, play, dance, or act it, either directly or by means of any device or process . . . ." (17 U.S.C. § 101 [1990]). Public performance is defined as "to perform or display it at a place open to the public or at any place where a substantial number of persons outside of a normal circle of a family and its social acquaintances is gathered; and (2) to transmit or otherwise communicate a performance or display of the work to a place specified by clause (1) . . . ." (17 U.S.C.§ 101 [1990]).

Fair use

Copyright law is intended to balance the rights of authors and artists against the right of the public to the free flow of ideas and information. Therefore, certain uses of copyrighted material are allowed without permission of the owner. These exceptions are granted mainly for the purposes of criticism, reviews, news reporting, research and scholarship, but there are also fair use provisions that apply to the performance of works. Exception (1) of Section 110 of the Copyright Act, states that permission of the copyright owner is not required for "performance . . . of a work by instructors or pupils in the course of face-to-face teaching activities of a nonprofit educational institution, in a classroom or similar place devoted to instruction." Janis Bruwelheide, writing in *The Copyright Primer for Librarians and Educators,* interprets this exception to include libraries and librarians. However, fair use in nonprofit educational institutions may not extend to performances by actors, singers or instrumentalists brought in from outside (Judiciary House Report No. 94-1476). Fair use also permits performance of works as a part of religious services, and at some very narrowly-defined charity events. The section of the law governing fair use exceptions for performances is reprinted in *The Copyright Primer for Librarians and Educators;* the entire fair use section and related information may be viewed on the World Wide Web at http://fairuse.stanford.edu/.

The public domain

Faced with the bewildering complications of copyright, many storytellers choose to tell only folktales that are in the public domain. A work is said to be in the public domain if copyright protection has expired. A work published in the U.S. at least seventy-five years ago is in the public domain, since under the present copyright law, any work created before 1978 is protected for a maximum of 75 years. For works published and copyrighted prior to 1978, protection expires on December 31 of the seventy-fifth year following publication. Certain works published before 1989 and within the past 75 years are in the public domain, if for example, the copyright was not renewed, as the law at that time required, or if the proper notice was not placed on the work. Many of the publications of the United States Government are in the public domain. For works created on or after January 1, 1978, the term of copyright is automatically the duration of the author's life plus fifty years. Determining which works published within the past 75 years are in the public domain is quite challenging, since many different criteria apply, however your search for a copyright owner may reveal that the work is not copyrighted. For a detailed explanation of the applicable laws, see *The Copyright Handbook*.

The U.S. copyright status of works published abroad has undergone changes since 1989, the year the U.S. signed the Berne Convention, governing international copyright. More recently, the GATT and NAFTA treaties have changed the U.S. copyright status for foreign works. Determining whether a work published abroad is in the public domain requires the assistance of a specialist in international copyright.

Copyright violation

Federal law provides serious penalties for copyright infringement (unauthorized copying of a work). Anyone who believes his or her work has been used illegally has the right to sue, and can be awarded actual damages, attorney fees, and statutory

damages of up to $100,000. A lawsuit against the average story-
teller does not seem likely; it's more probable that an unhappy
copyright owner would either demand that a teller cease and
desist from performing a particular tale, or ask for retroactive
compensation. Aside from legal complications, though, the
unauthorized teller of copyrighted material could encounter the
disapproval of her peers, or of sponsoring organizations such as
libraries that are careful about copyright compliance, and thus
damage her reputation. And if one day a teller wishes to record
an audio or videotape, or publish a collection of stories, compliance with copyright laws will be absolutely essential. It would be
foolish to spend time developing and perfecting a tale, and later
not be able to use it because of copyright problems.

How can anyone copyright a tale from the oral tra-dition?

In theory, this is a good question. The general plots and
motifs of oral traditional tales are old, and are common proper-
ty (in the public domain). However, most contemporary storytellers come across tales in print, or hear book tales told. The
problem for the storyteller then is to determine which parts of a
text are commonplace and traditional, and which represent the
work of the reteller. The more you know about folk traditions,
the easier it will be for you to determine which elements in a
work are traditional and which are the additions of the reteller.
A similar problem was addressed in the court case Bachman v.
Belasco (1915), which created what is called the "scenes en faire"
doctrine in copyright. The problem arises often in theater and
film: when is a situation is so common that anyone could have
thought of it? According to Bachman v. Belasco, "[if] a situation
is suggested by a common source, others, to whom the same situation 'naturally' presents itself are free to use it, provided that
the idea is obtained from the common source, not the copyrighted work of the prior user."

Many people don't understand the amount of work that is
required to make a tale from another time or culture come alive

for a modern audience. For a good example of the way a skilled reteller of folktales works, see *The Cat's Purr*, by Ashley Bryant (Atheneum, 1985). On the final page of the book, Bryant has reprinted the original ethnographic text from which he created his story. Though certainly rooted in folk tradition, *The Cat's Purr* is a unique artistic work, significantly expanded from a very spare tale indeed.

Be careful not to take at face value a book's claim to be "an old tale," words which serve as the subtitle of Tomie de Paola's picture book *Strega Nona* (Simon & Schuster, 1975). In an interview in *Storytelling Magazine*, de Paola stated,

> People are always surprised to find out that there is no such Italian folk tale. *Strega Nona* is an original copy-righted character, and her story is original, although it has antecedents in the porridge-pot and sea-is-salt type of stories. But the character is new and the setting is new. My publishers vigorously pursue those who use *Strega Nona* without permission! (Summer 1993, p. 19)

Because many retellers of folktales combine diverse elements from folk tradition, such as plot episodes, characters, customs and beliefs, with original material, a storyteller cannot merely paraphrase a copyrighted folktale text and claim that it is in the public domain.

Complying with copyright law

You can use a copyrighted tale provided you receive the permission of the copyright owner or designated agent. In other performing arts, there are established methods of facilitating this process. In the theater, for instance, publishers of playscripts collect standard royalties from play producers. The American Society of Composers, Artists and Publishers (ASCAP) oversees compensation to songwriters and musicians. Unfortunately, no established rate scale or mechanism for paying royalties exists for storytellers, leaving each teller to negotiate as best he can with publishers and authors. The process of obtaining permission can take a long time, and should be begun several months in advance of the date you will need it. If all goes well, you will obtain permission for a small fee, or free. In some cases, despite your best efforts, you may not be able to locate the copyright owner, or will not receive a reply.

The fact that you have tried every means possible to locate the owner of a copyright doesn't give you the legal right to use it, though it does make it unlikely that the copyright owner will ever find you. If you choose to tell a tale anyway, you should carefully document your efforts to locate the copyright owner, and be prepared to pay for permission if you do find one another. Hopefully storytellers' will one day be able to request and receive permission to use copyrighted material quickly and easily through some sort of central registry.

When not to ask permission

Before you request permission to tell a tale, make sure that text you have in hand is not in the public domain. You may suspect that an entire book is a reprint of an older work. Some publishing houses specialize in reprinting public domain books, and this should be evident from the information on the verso of the title page. A librarian can help you determine whether or not a book is a reprint, and its original publication date. If a tale in a collection was taken from a source that was protected by copyright at the time of printing, there should be a permission notice somewhere in the book. Anthologists are under no obligation to cite the sources of public domain tales, however, and many do not. I sometimes do not, because for some tales it would be too tedious to document every source I used—the source note would become as long as the story itself. An anthology of tales may include only a general list of sources, in which case you will have to try various strategies in order to match a particular tale to a bibliographic entry.

Often, a storyteller has to decide whether it will be easier to try to obtain permission from an anthologist, or to conduct a long and possibly fruitless search for the underlying source. It is certainly possible to write to an anthologist and request the name of a source. If you intend to claim that your telling comes from a particular source, such as a public domain work cited in another work, never fail to look at it! Some anthologists and retellers make radical changes in texts.

If you are planning to retell a tale using several different sources (which are not derived from a single copyrighted source) permission should not be necessary. Make sure that the tale elements you are using in your adaptation are traditional, and not unique artistic creations. The tale type and motif indexes listed in Chapter 3 are useful in verifying that tale plots, episodes and characters are traditional. Keep a record of all of your sources, in case you are challenged.

Obtaining permission to tell a copyrighted tale

A copyright owner can grant a storyteller permission to perform a work (tell a tale) by signing and dating a simple statement to that effect (see sample letters below). The term "nonexclusive permission" is sometimes used in order to indicate that others may be granted the right to perform the same work. In negotiating such a permission, the storyteller attempts to obtain the most unrestricted rights for the least amount of money. Permission should be granted for an unlimited period of time, either free or for a flat fee (and never on a per-performance basis). Permission to record or otherwise publish a work is a separate matter, and is not implied in a permission to perform.

It isn't possible to know who owns the copyright to a work simply by looking at the work itself. Copyright may be controlled by the publisher of the work, the author, the author's heirs or designated representative, such as a literary agent. Different kinds of rights, such as performance and translation rights, may be owned by different people.

Begin the process of seeking permission by writing to the publisher, provided they are still in business. Addresses of publishers can be found in the *Gale Directory of Publications* and *The Literary Market Place*. A librarian can help you find addresses of foreign publishers, and also trace publishers and journals that may have changed names or merged with others.

Permission requests should be typed on letterhead and addressed to the Rights and Permissions Department. Include a stamped, self-addressed envelope, or, for letters to foreign publishers, international response coupons, available from the Postal Service. If the publisher does not control the rights, they will usually provide you with the name and address of the person who does. Allow the publisher several weeks to respond, then follow up with a telephone call, and more letters if necessary.

Many publishers will grant permission to tell a story free of charge. However, since publishing companies do have to pay staff to handle permission requests, it is only fair that they charge a reasonable fee. As you wait for the publisher to respond to your request, calculate the cash value of that particular tale to you in terms of your ability to book performances, please your audiences, and enhance your reputation. Then you will know how much you are willing to pay. The copyright owner may ask for less, but if you are asked to pay a fee you consider too high, you can always make a counteroffer. Never plead poverty. Simply state that the fee exceeds your budget.

The following are some guidelines to follow in composing a permission request letter to a publisher:

• Provide the name of the author (editor, translator, etc.), title, date, place and publisher of the entire work; and the title and page numbers of the individual tale you wish to perform. Include a photocopy of the title page of the entire work, the page on which copyright notice is printed, the table of contents of the book, and the first page of the tale.

• Describe where and when (generally) you intend to perform the tale. It shouldn't be necessary to mention that you will be altering it slightly in performance, but if you will be making substantial changes, you can use the words "adapt for storytelling performance."

• If you want permission to use the story on an audiotape, videotape, book, etc. you must state when and by whom the work will be published, how many copies you will be producing, the retail price, and the tale's percentage of total content of the work you plan to produce.

• Ask what "credit line" you should include in printed material. Most publishers are particular about the wording of permission acknowledgements, since this brief text proclaims their copyright ownership.

• Don't make an offer of payment—after all, you may receive permission free of charge.

• Request that if the publishing company does not control the copyright, they send you the name and address of the person who does.

• Most publishers have their own subsidiary rights contract, but you should make it possible for a signed and returned copy of your letter to serve as permission, if the publisher so chooses. Many do, especially when granting permission free or for a small fee. Place the following at the bottom of your letter, substituting actual names:

Consented and agreed to:

_____   _____
(your name)   Date

_____   _____
For (publisher's name)   Date

Include a signed copy of the letter and your brochure. Hopefully, your brochure will convey to the copyright owner that you are professional enough to do justice to the material, yet are an independent artist who can't afford to pay more than a modest fee.

A letter to an author or anthologist should be more personal. By all means, explain why you want to retell the story. Often, the knowledge that the story will be shared with audiences is adequate compensation.

The Society of Children's Book Writers and Illustrators, in a pamphlet distributed to members in 1996 titled "Answers to

Some Questions about Contracts," offered its members this advice:

> There is also a growing number or storytellers who tour, generally locally, and tell stories, sometimes their own or public domain material, but also other people's work. Requests just to read or tell the story are generally granted for free but taping, either audio or visual, or other reproduction should not be allowed without compensation. And, be sure the storyteller plugs the book itself!

The following is a sample letter to an author:

Dear (author's name),

I am a storyteller, and I would like to request the nonexclusive right to tell your story [name of story] from the book [title, publisher and date] to [describe types of audiences]. I will acknowledge your book as the source of the tale, both during performances and in printed programs.

Your signature at the bottom of this letter will serve as permission to use your tale in live performances. I am enclosing a duplicate copy of this letter for your records.

Consented and agreed to:

_____   _____
(your name)   Date

_____   _____
(author's name)   Date

Be sure to enclose a stamped, self-addressed envelope, and a copy of your brochure. In some cases, copyright is controlled by the heirs of the author, which can make obtaining permission more difficult, since heirs are notoriously harder to find and to negotiate with than authors.

If you are unable to get a reply from a publisher, it is possible to request a search of the copyright records of the Library of Congress in order to find out the name of the registered owner of copyright. A search currently costs $20 per hour, and you can get an estimate of how much your search will cost by calling the Reference and Bibliography Section at 202-707-6850. For more information about copyright search, request Circular 22: How to Investigate the Copyright Status of a Work from the Copyright Office of the Library of Congress, Washington, D.C. 20559-6000. This circular is also available online. Records for works published since 1978 may be searched online by telnetting to locis.loc.gov and selecting the copyright menu, or via the Library of Congress at http://lcweb.loc.gov/copyright/. The copyright records may also be searched in person at the Library of Congress.

Because works may be protected by copyright law even if they were not registered with the Library of Congress, a copyright search alone will not prove conclusively that a work is in the public domain.

Ethics and storytelling

If you wish to tell a story you hear from another storyteller you should always discuss this with the teller. Bear in mind, however, that a storyteller's permission to tell a tale doesn't guarantee that the tale is not from a copyrighted source. It's possible that the tale is copyrighted, and it is also possible it is a common tale that you could find in print and adapt in your own way. For the text of a spirited online discussion of story rights and copyright, see the ethics thread of the Storytell listserv, best accessed via the Storytelling Home Page on the World Wide Web at http://members.aol.com/storypage/. Select "best of Storytell," then "the ethics of storytelling."

After reading through this long discussion of rights, you may well wonder about the rights of the people who shared their tales with the folklorists, anthropologists and others, and the collective rights of a group of people to their oral traditional tales. This has only recently become an important issue among folklorists. Over the past fifty years, fieldworkers have become more scrupulous about including traditional tellers' analyses and explanations of tales in published work, and have even collaborated with them as co-authors of books and articles.

The United Nations Educational and Scientific Organization (UNESCO) has urged U.N. member states to "co-operate closely so as to ensure internationally that the various interested parties (communities or natural or legal persons) enjoy the economic, moral and so called neighbouring rights resulting from the investigation, creation, composition, performance, recording and/or dissemination of folklore" (*Recommendation on the Safeguarding of Traditional Culture and Folklore adopted by the General Conference of Unesco at its 25th Session,* Paris, France, 17 October to 16 Novermber, 1989). It remains to be seen whether these recommendations will have an effect on copyright laws. At the present time, the decision of how to acknowledge and repay those who originated and shaped traditional oral narratives rests with each storyteller.

INDEX

AUTHORS

TITLES